GAMING LIFE

Living an Authentic Faith in a Conflicted Culture

Jim Bettison

BLOOMIN' PEN PUBLISHING

BELLFOWER, MISSOURI

Paperback — ISBN: 979-8-9888520-4-9

Kindle Edition — ISBN: 979-8-9888520-5-6

E-PUB — ISBN: 979-8-9888520-6-3

Library of Congress Control Number: 2024918051

Printed in the United States of America

WHAT ARE PEOPLE SAYING

ABOUT GAMING LIFE BY JIM BETTISON?

"A clever, insightful, and relevant Bible Study. The use of modern gaming terminology will pique the interest of gamers (like me) and non-gamers alike. Jim's writing is easy to read but comes packed with a deep understanding of Biblical truth and how it can be applied to people's lives today. Your small group will love this book."

— Gabriel Phifer, BS Aeronautical & Astronautical Engineering, MIT '03

"Gaming Life is a great read! And while it may connect in a special way with gamers, the content is sure to resonate with anyone who wants to stop playing games with their faith and grow as an authentic follower of Jesus."

— Jeff Hogan, Lead Pastor at Convergence Christian Church (C3)

"I found Gaming Life to wonderfully parallel the Christian journey with the characteristics of a MMO/RPG game vs the outlook that we have while serving Christ. This book helps to identify those stages of the journey that we are struggling in. No matter if we are leveling up, or fighting scripted monsters in caves, our GM God has provided the key to victory with his word and the ultimate reward of eternal life when our game ends."

—James Pryor, Troop Ministry Liaison, Trail Life USA.

ACKNOWLEDGMENTS

I am indebted to my wife, Karen, lovely inside and out, who embodies the love, grace, wisdom, and truth that make me a better man, and this a better book.

I am grateful for my dad, George Bettison, whose affection for God's Word inspired me even before I decided to follow Jesus.

I must mention Professor Keith McCaslin and Dr. William Baker, who opened the Bible to me and helped me finally begin understanding God's Word.

Special thanks to

Dr. Don Sanders

Joshua Bettison

For the word of God is living and active
and sharper than any two-edged sword,
and piercing as far as the division of soul
and spirit, of both joints and marrow,
and able to judge the thoughts
and intentions of the heart.

(Hebrews 4:12 NASB)

CONTENTS

CONTENTS

FOREWORD

Embarking on a spiritual journey is a lot like diving into a new video game, and "Gaming Life" by Jim Bettison brilliantly maps out this journey. From the opening chapter, the book immerses you in a quest of profound discovery and growth, much like entering an expansive open-world game.

Jim uses his personal experiences and other examples journeying through the narrative, filled with challenges, triumphs, and crucial checkpoints of faith. Just as in a game where you encounter various levels and bosses, this book walks you through real-life obstacles and victories, offering wisdom and guidance that acts as your spiritual power-ups.

Every chapter is akin to a new level, each with its own set of trials and rewards. Jim's reflections and insights serve as powerful tools, helping you navigate your own path with a stronger sense of purpose and divine guidance. The book's approach makes the spiritual journey engaging and relatable, drawing parallels with the experiences and growth one undergoes in a game.

Although I've started the main quest line in pursuing a relationship with Jesus, I feel like I'm not making much progress. I keep track of where I'm at within the storyline, however, I've been skirting alongside the main path getting too focused on side quests. "Gaming Life" provided me with some valuable new perspectives.

"Gaming Life" is not your typical full step-by-step walk-through; it's a guide that encourages you to level-up your relationship with Jesus, strategize your spiritual life, and appreciate the beauty of the quest you're on. It's a reminder that, much like in any epic adventure, every challenge faced is an opportunity to grow stronger and closer to God.

If you've ever felt like your spiritual walk needed a fresh perspective or a new set of strategies, this book is a great guide to leveling up your faith in a way that's both insightful and exhilarating.

-- Chris Stine, SGT USMC

INTRODUCTION

Gaming Life. It may sound weird, even misleading. This book contains no tips about gaining an advantage over co-workers, circumventing the Führer of your neighborhood HOA, or perfecting your 360 no-scope in Fortnite. Instead, it uses video game culture as a springboard to pursue a more authentic walk of faith.

We have come a long way since Atari released Pong in 1972. As captivating as Pong was to kids when it came out, it has long since lost its appeal to modern games with greater complexities, strategies, and immersive graphics.

Video games are more popular than ever. Some people look down on them, but many love them. Some are so addicted that they will wear diapers to avoid having to pause.

Good luck getting THAT image out of your head!

Whether you enjoy video games or not, we have something to learn from them.

The most popular games nowadays are Role-Playing Games (RPGs), where you step into a character's role. It's like playing a part in a movie. You control your character's decisions and actions to develop their skills and abilities. Many RPGs are First-Person Shooter (FPS) games, where you might be trying to shoot bad guys in a military-themed simulation or obliterating monsters trying to take over the world.

However, not every RPG is limited to being an FPS game. Your objective may be accumulating objects, racking up points, putting yourself in advantageous positions, or gaining more power and new skills. You might pilot a jet, drive a race car, or sneak around a dystopian city to rescue people or deliver goodies. Or maybe you're just looking for money.

Many role-playing games are merely shoot 'em up, cheap-thrill games. But other games have more imaginative creators who inspire us with intriguing storylines and complex situations to resolve, making us strategically manage resources to survive, thrive, or embark on various adventures.

What does this have to do with our faith or walk as followers of Jesus Christ? Well, I grew up in a churchgoing family, but we weren't Christians. And we rubbed elbows with many churchgoers who were a lot like us. As far back as I can remember, most churchgoers I've known are like first-person shooters in a role-playing game. We navigated through the levels of church life, gaining points and resolving situations. Then, we "paused the action" and returned to our regular lives, which had little to do with our church life or faith.

Maybe you understand what I'm saying. Perhaps you don't. Let's go ahead and hit play!

CHAPTER ONE

GAMING CHURCH

Every Sunday morning, a Christian, let's call him Rusty, steps into a character's role — the churchgoer. He navigates through all the elements of church life, managing his resources, saying and doing the right things at the right time, developing skills, racking up points, positioning himself advantageously, and so on. Maybe he's after the perks of survival (not going to hell). Perhaps he's trying to upgrade his skills to be a "better Christian" (mastering church jargon and shouting "amen" at the right time). Or, he may enjoy the adventure: the preaching, the music, the fellowship, or even the doughnuts and coffee.

Then, when church is over, Rusty steps out of the "churchgoer" role and returns to his "normal" life, which has little to do with God. When he goes to church, he's different. He is Church Rusty. When he's at home, at work, or in other social situations, he's Everyday Rusty. He has integrated his faith only into his church life, not into the other parts of his life. Nevertheless, Rusty considers himself a Christian.

Many churchgoers are merely avatars in an RPG called "Church Life." Perhaps that sounds judgmental, but listen:

If you are "gaming" church, going through the motions to look like and act like a Christian on Sunday morning, but the real you is a worldly person at home, at work, or play, then you are also "gaming" God.

One family decided to do what the preacher said in his sermon and introduce someone to Jesus. So they invited their neighbors to dinner one night. It was time for the meal, and the hostess decided to show their neighbors how well they upheld Christian standards in their home. So she asked five-year-old Johnny to say grace. Little Johnny was a bit shy. "I don't know what to say." Awkward pause. The mother continued smiling, "Well, sweetheart, just say what Daddy says, like he did at breakfast this morning."

And that's when little Johnny said, "Oh God, we've got those awful people coming to dinner tonight."[1]

It's like what George Burns said, "The key to success is sincerity. If you can fake that, you've got it made."[2]

None of us need fake sincerity — we have politicians and journalists for that. But I'll tell you where you can go if you want to be an authentic Christian, and that's the Bible. And I believe an ideal place to start is the Sermon on the Mount.

SALT

In Matthew chapter five, Jesus said:

> *You are the salt of the earth; but if the salt has become tasteless, how can it be made salty again? It is no longer good for anything, except to be thrown out and trampled under foot by men.* (Matthew 5:13, NASB)

Jesus used this metaphor to teach us something. He said, ***"You are the salt of the earth ..."*** We know salt makes things taste better. Once you've enjoyed fries with salt, it's hard to tolerate them without it. People back in Jesus' day also used salt for flavor, but it was primarily used as a preservative. You could pack meat or fish in salt, and it would prevent it from going bad as quickly. So salt is very good — we get that.

Ever gotten salt in a wound? We now have ointments for wounds, so no one uses salt for that anymore. But you can put salt on a wound, and it will help heal it. Salt speeds up osmosis, and it can kill germs that cause infection. But, salt in a wound stings like all get out, even if it is good.

When Jesus says, **"YOU ARE the salt of the earth"** (emphasis mine), he's using plural language. He's speaking to many people — the entire body of his followers.

That's a critical distinction. You see, we all too often think it's just "me." We think we're first-person shooters in a role-playing game, but we're not. The church is an assembly of followers of Jesus, not a building or individual. Rather than a first-person shooter, the church resembles a Massively Multiplayer Online Role-Playing Game (MMORPG, or MMO for short). What distinguishes an MMO is that many people from all over the globe can interact on the same server.

I want to point out that we, the church, are a community unlike any other community on earth. We interact on the local level and global level — on the same server, so to speak — in the spiritual dimension as well as in the physical dimension of our cultures. So when Jesus says, **"YOU"** (plural) **"are the salt of the earth"** (emphasis mine), he's referring to us as a multi-member people-of-God community, unified by God's Word, God's Spirit, and the shared objective to preserve and cleanse.

But if each of us is "gaming" church — merely adopting a Christian persona — then there's a problem. Rusty is our churchgoer who faithfully shows up to church. He knows how to greet fellow churchgoers and how much time he has for his doughnut and coffee before taking a seat. He knows how to sing the songs, bow his head, and pass the communion tray and offering plate. Maybe he even amens during the sermon. He has adopted a Christian persona that more or less disappears when he leaves the church building. The church is up to its gills with men like Rusty — men who know how to LOOK Christian but don't know how to BE Christian.

We grimace at the politician who shows up at a soup kitchen for a photo opportunity but cares little about the poor. No one wants a repairman who just LOOKS like a repairman. We want one who will DO the work. No one wants a server who only LOOKS like a server. We want one who will SERVE us. God desires his children — citizens of his kingdom — to SERVE him and DO the work of the kingdom. Jesus said, " ... *if the salt has become tasteless, how can it be made salty again? It is no longer good for anything ... "* (Matthew 5:13 NASB). And that is pretty sobering. We all understand this: if you put salt on your fries but found they weren't salty, you'd get rid of whatever was in that shaker. When you go through the motions, merely LOOKING like a Christian without SERVING the kingdom or DOING the work of the kingdom, you've lost your flavor.

LIGHT

When Jesus said, **"You are the light of the world,"** he introduced another metaphor: light. In the Bible, light often represents truth, understanding, and wisdom.

> *You are the light of the world. A city set on a hill cannot be hidden; nor does anyone light a lamp and put it under a basket, but on the lampstand, and it gives light to all who are in the house.* (Matthew 5:14-15 NASB)

When I was a teen, I was horsing around in a friend's front yard and lost my dad's car keys. It was dark so we looked with flashlights but couldn't find them. I got a ride home and had to explain to Dad why we had no car. The following day, I returned, and in the morning light, I found the keys within thirty seconds. That's a good illustration of searching for truth with man's light versus God's light. Anyway, that's what light does — it illuminates! And the better the light, the better it illuminates.

Jesus said:

> *Let your light shine before men in such a way that they may see your good works, and glorify your Father who is in heaven.* (Matthew 5:16, NASB)

If you are going to let your light shine, then what you need to have is — the light! John Chapter 1 tells us:

> *In him was life, and the life was the light of*
> *men.* (John 1:4 NASB)

That light is the wisdom and truth of Jesus Christ. You can't shine a light you don't possess, so stepping into Christian character — like a gamer in a role-playing game — and going through the motions on Sunday morning isn't going to get that understanding, wisdom, or truth of the Gospel into you.

There was a little boy named Mikey who went to church with his parents the day they had a baby dedication ceremony for his newborn brother. Mikey sobbed all the way home in the back seat. His father asked him many times what was wrong. Finally, Mikey replied, "That preacher said he wanted us kids brought up in a Christian home, but I want to stay with you guys."[3]

You can't game church, and you can't game God. I mean, really, you can't even game Mikey! What does Jesus expect of us if we are to let our light shine so they — whoever "they" are — may see and glorify God? People cannot see the wisdom and truth of Jesus Christ. They can only see how you live out that wisdom and truth. The truth of the Gospel can only be lived out when you decide to turn away from playing the game and turn toward being an authentic follower of Jesus Christ. You can act like a Christian, or you can be a Christian — those are radically different. Even you and Mikey know that, so you can be sure no one is fooling God.

SALT & LIGHT

Light is a beautiful thing. We love seeing the lights of cities when we're flying over them at night. Or gazing into the eyes of your true love. Or driving by houses ablaze with brilliant Christmas lights. One of the most magnificent things I've seen was when my submarine surfaced in the middle of the ocean at night. The stars were breathtaking. But when the sun dawned on the horizon, it was like we were on another planet, surrounded by purple, blue, pink, and orange pearlescence. It was beyond beautiful.

Light is indeed beautiful, but it's also practical — like when I needed to find my keys. Or when you're reading a book. Or navigating unfamiliar roads. So yes, light is great, but don't forget: light also exposes.

Many people like to stay in the dark because they fear certain truths may come to light. That keeps many of us in the dark, too. But we need Jesus to apply salt to our wounds and shine light in our dark corners. Sure, his salt will sting, but our wounds won't heal without him. And yes, his light is offensive, but until he exposes our lies and dark secrets, we'll keep those sins hidden, and they will remain a barrier between us and the

Lord (Isaiah 59:2). Those sins will keep his light from shining in you, keep you Gaming Church, and prevent you from being the light of the world.

THE CHURCH

This is an uncomfortable read. Read it anyway. Yes, you have some things in you and clinging to you that you need Jesus to root out and cleanse. But God has blessed you with this magnificent community called the church. Some of you don't like church and don't go because hypocrites are there. Churches indeed have hypocrites. But whether you are in a church, a grocery store, a bar, a school, or a repair shop, you can't throw a stick without hitting a hypocrite. However, the church, unlike all those other places, is a unique community that is life-changing because of Jesus Christ and his salt and light.

Most people think you can be a spiritually healthy, mature Christian without ever going to church, and that isn't true. Jesus said, *"You"* (plural) *"are the salt of the earth."* There's no such thing as "a salt." Salt is thousands and millions of grains of salt. We are the salt of the earth; we preserve and heal when we pour ourselves out.

> You are the light of the world. A city set on a hill cannot be hidden. (Matthew 5:14 NASB)

Tell me, when is one person a city? Never. You'll never be a city all by yourself. Jesus refers to you as an assembly of his followers. The Bible calls that the church. It's not a building; it's a dynamic organism made up of people following the Lord and abiding in him.

ELEMENTS OF SPIRITUAL HEALTH

We identify three elements that contribute to a person's spiritual health. The first is the WORSHIP element — that's what we do in a worship service in a church building or someone's home, but it is not limited to those places. We show God we love him by singing to him, singing about him, reading and hearing from his Word, praying, taking the Lord's Supper, and even giving tithes and offerings. Of course, worship is not limited to those activities.

The second is the DISCIPLESHIP element. This describes activities such as Sunday morning Bible study, mid-week small group, personal time studying God's Word, spending time in prayer, and so on.

The third is the SERVING element. Helping others, greeting, mowing, serving communion, cleaning up, helping at a nursing home, being useful in the community, and so forth.

You recognize that some of these activities are done individually, but Christians do many things together —

worshiping, serving, and discipling. This is by design. It is essential for Christians to come together because the community of Jesus-followers facilitates all these elements and catalyzes the transformation God is working in us. We help one another in the church to become salt and light. All together, we follow Jesus, who shone his beautiful and exposing light in us and is the preserving, disinfecting salt who poured himself out for us, reconciling us to himself. Now, we carry on his ministry of reconciliation (2 Corinthians 5:18), being salt and light to the world.

At the end of the Beatitudes, Jesus said:

> *Blessed are you when people insult you and persecute you, and falsely say all kinds of evil against you because of Me.* (Matthew 5:11 NASB)

You don't feel blessed when people revile and persecute you. In fact, almost all of the Beatitude statements seem upside-down. We feel blessed when people like us and say good things about us, but Jesus said we have that wrong.

We know salt flavors and preserves. We know light illuminates. We love that. But we also know salt stings and light exposes. When you live by God's Word — living as the salt of the earth and the light of the world — there is something attractive about it. At the same time, there is something offensive about it.

You have heard well-meaning Christians complain that all the world knows is what Christians are against. Of course, no one wants to listen to someone drone on about everything wrong with the world. You've also heard unbelievers rail against Christians who "try to tell everyone how they should live their lives."

Well? Are we supposed to be kind-hearted and gentle toward everyone? Or should we take a stand for what is good, right, and holy? My answer is: of course!

If we are good at living as the salt of the earth and the light of the world, then there will be something both attractive and offensive about it. Admittedly, it takes a lot of maturity to become good at being salt and light.

Peter alludes to this in 1 Peter 4.

> *If you are reviled for the name of Christ,*
> *you are blessed, because the Spirit of glory*
> *and of God rests on you. Make sure that*
> *none of you suffers as a murderer, or thief,*
> *or evildoer, or a troublesome meddler.*
> (1 Peter 4:14-15 NASB)

If people get ticked off because you're the obnoxious one telling them they're screwed up and going to hell, then they might be rightly upset at you. All too often, Christians let their emotions get the better of them. They grow angry, and then they get salty in a worldly way instead of the Jesus way.

For 2000 years, Christians have lived and thrived in societies that are hostile to God and his Word. We will survive and thrive, too, as long as we are salt and light.

Being salt and shining your light so others will see your good works and glorify God mean you will pour yourself out in various ways. It means you will show compassion, serve, and come alongside others like Jesus and the disciples did. That shows people the hope we possess and also the love, grace, and mercy that make such a difference in us.

Sometimes, being salt and shining your light mean presenting the truth or opposing lies, manipulation, and evil. Taking a stand for what is good and right will put you at odds with those who love darkness. To boot, refusing to compromise your principles often offends. After all, salt also stings, and light also exposes.

That's not what people do when they are gaming church, though. Churchgoers tend to be overly concerned that others like them. They will often compromise their beliefs and principles and may even lie to ensure they don't become unpopular. They tend to remain silent instead of speaking truth into someone else's life for fear of being disliked.

Authentic Christians are individual followers of Jesus Christ, together as the church, intentionally living in the world, pouring themselves out, and shining their light for the glory of God.

We have an extraordinarily imaginative Creator who inspires us with his love, grace, and mercy — with the truth of how he poured himself out for us to preserve us and heal us. We have his light because he endured the darkness of suffering and death for us. Now, the light of his Word and his Spirit enable us to survive and thrive no matter what "adventures" we face.

DISCUSSION & REFLECTION

1. Describe a situation where the lack of light (either literal or figurative) put you at a disadvantage.

    ✗ What did you learn from that situation?

    ✗ Did you do anything to prevent that situation from happening again?

2. Recount a time when someone confronted you with a truth that was hard for you to hear.

    ✗ How did you feel? Offended? Humbled?

    ✗ Did you act on that truth? How?

3. Rate how often you shine light to others. 1 = never, 10 = every chance you get.

   1 — 2 — 3 — 4 — 5 — 6 — 7 — 8 — 9 — 10

4. What changes could you make to raise that score?

5. What areas of church life do you struggle with "going through the motions?"

6. Has involvement in a Christian community ever impacted your walk with God? How?

   ✗ Has a lack of such involvement ever impacted you? How?

7. Between Worship, Discipleship, and Service, which is the easiest for you to get involved in? Which is the hardest? Does the presence of other people make it easier?

8. Describe a situation where you felt tension between social pressure and your Christian principles.

9. Have your Christian principles ever put you at a disadvantage? At work? At home? At school?

_____ Chapter 1 Notes

[1] Just the Truth - Hypocrites Jokes. http://jokes.christiansunite.com/Hypocrites/
Just_the_Truth.shtml

[2] Goodreads.com. https://www.goodreads.com/quotes/7132775-the-key-to-success-is-sincerity-if-you-can-fake

[3] Jollynotes.com. https://www.jollynotes.com/christian-humor-christian-jokes-clean-jokes
-best-christian-jokes/

CHAPTER TWO

GAMING NAMES

In the Bible, most names carry a meaning. Peter means rock; Abraham means father of a multitude; Jesus' name is Yeshua, which means Yahweh Saves. Other names sound similar to something. Samuel's name sounds like Hebrew for "heard of God" because his mother understood God had heard her prayer.

A person's name is associated with his character and integrity. When people say, "He made a name for himself," it means he succeeded. When people hear his name, they think, "He made it big." You see how his success has become part of his identity.

It happens the other way around, too. People would associate his name with his misfortune if he lost everything instead.

Certain attributes come to mind whenever you hear someone's name. Maybe you think "smart" or "not-so-smart," "honest" or "dishonest," "kind" or "judgmental," "generous" or "stingy." Maybe your name doesn't carry a specific meaning like biblical names do, but your name IS associated with your character.

Gamers create or are assigned usernames on various platforms. Sometimes, the app randomly generates those usernames, but you can usually choose your own. Usernames, or tags, communicate something to others who see it, whether we like it or not. The "something" that your username communicates will be associated with you. What might your tag say to others about you?

JOSEPH

In Genesis, we read about Joseph. He was a bit spoiled. Jacob, his father, favored him, lavishing him with special treatment and gifts. On top of that, Joseph made a name for himself among his older siblings as an arrogant, boasting tattletale. His behavior irked his brothers to no end, and they betrayed Joseph, selling him to some passing traders. A high-ranking Egyptian official named Potiphar bought Joseph to be his slave.

Humbled, he began making a name for himself at Mr. Potiphar's estate. He still conducted himself with the faith in Yahweh he learned from his father. He worked hard for his Egyptian master and excelled to the point that Mr. Potiphar put him in charge of everything.

> *It came about after these events that his master's wife looked with desire at Joseph, and she said, "Lie with me." But he refused and said to his master's wife, "Behold, with me here, my master does not concern himself with anything in the house, and he has put all that he owns in my charge. There is no one greater in this house than I, and he has withheld nothing from me except you, because you are his wife. How then could I do this great evil and sin against God?"* (Genesis 39:7-9 NASB)

Snubbed, Potiphar's wife accused Joseph of rape. Mr. Potiphar threw Joseph in prison. And right there in the dungeon, Joseph established the very first prison ministry! I believe Mr. Potiphar knew that attempted rape was contrary to Joseph's reputation — his name — and that's why he put Joseph in prison instead of executing him.

Joseph made a name for himself even in prison. He was diligent in his work, his integrity shone brightly, and he gained a reputation for interpreting dreams. And that contributed to Joseph's rise to power in Egypt. Remarkably, when he had the opportunity to do so, he didn't retaliate against his brothers who had betrayed him. That's how we remember Joseph — we associate his name with his gifts, leadership, and integrity.

DANIEL

The prophet Daniel was a youth when he was taken captive to Babylon. He and his companions respectfully refused to eat the food assigned to them because that food had been offered to idols. As a result, their Babylonian attendants recognized them as forthcoming and honest.

Kings and officials of three world empires recognized Daniel's character and integrity. Even Daniel's enemies knew he was a man of exceptional character. Fearing Daniel would receive a higher rank than they, these wise guys sought to get him out of the picture.

> Then these men said, "We will not find any ground of accusation against this Daniel unless we find it against him with regard to the law of his God." (Daniel 6:5 NASB)

Daniel's enemies manipulated the king to sign a mandate saying no one was allowed to pray to anyone but the king, but

Daniel continued to pray to Yahweh. That's how we remember Daniel — we associate his name with his honesty and steadfast faith in God.

THE OTHER JOSEPH

In the New Testament, when Joseph learned Mary was pregnant before they were married, he wanted to divorce her. But, in mercy, he wished to avoid a scandal. He was concerned with the "name" or integrity of her family as well as his own.

PAUL

When the Apostle Paul came to Lystra with Barnabas, he healed a man crippled since birth. The witnesses thought Paul and Barnabas were gods and got ready to worship and sacrifice to them. Paul and Barnabas had the opportunity to make out big. Instead, they denied the assertions that they were divine and gave credit for the miracle to their Lord Jesus Christ. Paul consistently showed tremendous character and integrity. He was honest even when it put him at a disadvantage. Paul worked day and night so he would not be a burden to new church members and leaders. Wherever he went, his reputation preceded him. When people heard Paul's name, they recognized his excellence of character.

GOD

Character attributes also come to mind with titles. When God appeared to Moses from the midst of the burning bush, he said:

> *I am the God of your father, the God of Abraham, the God of Isaac, and the God of Jacob.* (Exodus 3:6 NASB)

The title God identified himself with was significant, and it communicated a world of information to Moses. Then Moses said to God:

> *"If I come to the people of Israel and say to them, 'The God of your fathers has sent me to you,' and they ask me, 'What is his name?' what shall I say to them?" God said to Moses, "I AM WHO I AM." And he said, "Say this to the people of Israel, 'I AM has sent me to you.'"* (Exodus 3:13-14 ESV)

This title, "I AM," also communicated a wealth of information to Moses — more than it does to us. Moses lived in a world filled with idols made of wood, stone, and metal, but they weren't real gods. However, Yahweh really is God — thus, he calls himself "I AM" because he is the only God.

However, after God brought the Israelites out of Egypt, he changed how he referred to himself. Oh, he's still the Great I AM, but he declared to the Israelites:

> *"I am Yahweh your God, who brought you out of the land of Egypt, out of the house of bondage."* (Exodus 20:2 WEB)

He demonstrated his powerful, loving, redeeming nature by bringing the Israelites out of Egypt with never-before-seen powers, plagues, and miracles. The way he refers to himself associates his name with his character and integrity.

JESUS

I already talked about Jesus' name, Yeshua, but He also carries a title. He is the **Son of God**. Remember how Satan spoke to him in the desert?

> *"IF you ARE the Son of God ... "* (Matthew 4:3 NASB, emphasis mine)

The very first thing Satan did was to call Jesus' name into question. He was trying to debuff or downgrade Jesus' character and integrity.

Politicians often do the same thing with their opponents. If anyone on the "other" side does what they don't like, then they smear, accuse, and paint the other's character and integrity with all the sludge they can.

Satan was audacious enough to call the character and integrity of the Son of God into question — to his face, even! — and you should know he will try the same thing with you.

NERFING

Something Satan likes to do is what the gaming world calls "Nerfing." When playing a character in an RPG, let's say you have a mega-laser that can destroy the game's monsters in one blast. But then the devs drastically decrease the laser's damage and accuracy; now, it's a mini-laser.

Imagine you needed to protect your home, so you open your gun cabinet only to find out there's a Nerf gun instead of your shotgun. That is undoubtedly where the term "Nerf" came from! It means you're weakened! Ineffective!

It's annoying when your weapon or character gets nerfed in a role-playing game, but it's detrimental in real life. You can be demoted or laid off. Now you're making less money or have to look for a new job. Your car can break down. Now, you find yourself less independent than you used to be.

Injury and illness can nerf you, too. My dear friend and colleague had a thriving ministry overseas as a missionary. One day, he discovered he had brain cancer. Over the next several years, his ability to function slowly deteriorated, making it impossible to carry out his ministry.

They say whatever doesn't kill you makes you stronger. But, like cancer, the devil's many schemes threaten to nerf us permanently.

IGNORANCE

But what things make a Christian weak? All sorts of things! Like ignorance. Paul lamented that many Jews did not believe in Jesus and attributed that to ignorance. He wrote:

> *For being ignorant of God's righteousness, and seeking to establish their own righteousness, they didn't subject themselves to the righteousness of God.* (Romans 10:3 WEB)

The Book of Hebrews was written to Jewish Christians who were considering reverting to Judaism. They thought of turning back primarily because of their ignorance. The author wrote:

> *Therefore lift your drooping hands and strengthen your weak knees, and make straight paths for your feet, so that what is lame may not be put out of joint but rather be healed.* (Hebrews 12:12-13 ESV)

This is particularly meaningful to me because I'm an amputee. After my leg was amputated, I had to relearn how to walk. Two -legged people don't have too much trouble navigating stairs, uneven terrain, or objects in their way. But those are more difficult for people using crutches or artificial limbs.

Spiritually, however, every one of us has handicaps: shortcomings, sins, addictions, hang-ups because of trauma, pain, shame, and so on — it's a very long list.

Just as an amputee needs physical therapy to overcome the challenges of walking with hardware, we need training to overcome our long list of issues so we can walk well with Jesus in this world full of hazards. Like it or not, we all face a steep learning curve.

They say what you don't know can't hurt you. Real life tells us this is not true. Not knowing there's cholera in the water? Not knowing your food is coated with herbicide and insecticide residues? See what I mean?

I grew up playing in Coldwater Creek, not knowing radioactive waste had been dumped there decades earlier. Now, many friends of mine are dead from cancer. What you don't know can definitely harm you.

Modern Christians tend to have little Bible knowledge. Kids who grew up knowing Jesus loves them show up at universities nowadays unprepared for confrontations with unbelievers. Atheist academics have studied more how to punch holes in their faith than these oblivious churchgoers ever studied God's Word or how to defend it.

It's most apparent when our young folks head off to college, but it happens to grown-ups, too. Even if a churchgoer is confident in WHAT he believes, he often does not know WHY he believes. When challenged on their beliefs, the typical response is, "I don't know." And what a powerful effect chuckles and mockery have on a churchgoer who is ignorant.

DEBUFF

Let's look, once again, at our churchgoer. Rusty believes in God, Jesus, and the Bible. He was baptized and went to church regularly. Maybe Rusty went to Sunday school as a child, but, like most churchgoers, he never participates in a Bible study.[4] His lack of biblical knowledge is a "debuff" that makes him weak and ineffective in his faith.

Now Rusty's new at college, hoping to be popular with his peers, praying to impress his profs, and counting on meeting that special someone. When an upperclassman poses a question about his faith that Rusty doesn't know how to answer, he nerfs Rusty's confidence. When a professor rants against Christians in his class, he debuffs Rusty's faith. Rusty is embarrassed to let anyone know he's a Christian.

All of Satan's minions are "griefing" Rusty: sabotaging, distressing, and frustrating him any way they can. They're chuckling, mocking, and nerfing him down to a little weakling. After all the debuffs pile up, Satan steps in to make the Kill Shot by tossing an attractive girl in front of him.

SIN

That's another thing that makes us weak. No, not attractive women, but sin!

Paul wrote:

> Don't you know that when you present
> yourselves as servants and obey someone,
> you are the servants of whomever you
> obey; whether of sin to death, or of
> obedience to righteousness? (Romans 6:16
> WEB)

Paul said you're either a slave to sin or a slave to righteousness.

So, our student Rusty has been nerfed and is at a weak point. He also has an opportunity for sin with "hot lips." His new "friends" tell him not to be a fuddy-duddy; he'd be crazy not to; everyone's doing it — all the modern slogans they love to toss around. So Rusty abandons his moral sensibilities and gives in to his lust. And he has opened the door and let Satan right in. He has nerfed himself.

Sexual sin is a big one and easier to use as our modern-day culture oozes downhill, but it is far from the only arrow in Satan's quiver. Satan will also present opportunities for greed, lying, cheating, and substance abuse to trip up ignorant churchgoers like Rusty. But that's not all.

CHEESING

We all have that one friend who loves taking advantage of glitches or oversights in a game's programming. He's "Cheesing": using odd or cheap strategies to beat everyone else's normal, civilized playstyle. Well, Satan cheeses, too. When we're low, he'll throw cheap shots at every opportunity.

So, maybe it's not a girl he uses to take Rusty out. Perhaps it's the death of a family member. That's a popular one. But there's also the loss of a job, the end of a friendship, the breakdown of a car, or an accident. How about everything getting stolen out of Rusty's dorm room? Satan loves to cheese — especially when you're ignorant and don't perceive what he's doing.

Again, Satan doesn't cheese only young folks. He does it to grown-ups all the time. Less than half of a typical congregation attends any kind of Bible study.[5] Ignorance, sin, and laziness all nerf you — and that creates the perfect opportunity for Satan to cheese.

If you spoke with an atheist, could you explain what you believe? Or why you believe? Could you defend your beliefs against the common slogans tossed around today? Can you explain why they're wrong when they say, "The Bible is unreliable"? Do you know why all religions cannot lead to God or heaven or why only Christianity can? Most Christians cannot answer these questions.

If you're unsure you can answer such questions, it doesn't mean you're not saved, but it does mean you're nerfed. This is not a good position to be in because it means you're ineffective and vulnerable. Paul wrote:

> ... we have not ceased to pray for you, asking that you may be filled with the knowledge of his will in all spiritual wisdom and understanding, so as to walk in a manner worthy of the Lord, fully pleasing to him, bearing fruit in every good work and increasing in the knowledge of God. (Colossians 1:9-10 ESV)

God has called us — commissioned us! — to make disciples (Matthew 28:18-20). There is Kingdom work to do, but many never get around to doing it because they can't seem to get past their issues or rise above their current levels of understanding. Living "nerfed" will not fill us with the knowledge of God's will, spiritual wisdom, or understanding. Remaining ignorant keeps us ineffective and vulnerable and prevents us from walking in a manner worthy of the Lord, bearing fruit, and increasing in the knowledge of God.

Most churches have Bible studies for children and adults in addition to the Sunday morning worship service, and many have midweek Bible studies. Statistics vary significantly about how many churchgoers participate in Bible study, but few Christians take advantage of the available opportunities to "buff" their faith.

In his wisdom, Peter wrote:

> *But in your hearts regard Christ the Lord as holy, always being prepared to make a defense to anyone who asks you for a reason for the hope that is in you;* (1 Peter 3:15 ESV)

But many merely want Jesus to save them; they're not interested in Jesus being their Lord and King or regarding him as holy. They don't see a need to study God's Word and defend their faith. Yet, as Peter says, it is essential to understand God's Word and how to defend it. Peter goes on to say:

> Yet do it with gentleness and respect, having a good conscience, so that, when you are slandered, those who revile your good behavior in Christ may be put to shame. (1 Peter 3:15-16 ESV)

Unfortunately, too many churchgoers remain ignorant of God's Word and slip-slide around instead of standing firm. They have unwittingly given themselves a bad name. Satan has many helpers on his side who would love to nerf you. In other words, they will point out your shortcomings, humiliate you, marginalize you, and make you look like a fool. And it's pretty easy for them to do that because American Christianity is nerfed. It has a bad name — its character, integrity, and reputation are in poor condition.

And when we play the religion game like that, it games the name of our Lord and Savior. When Christians don't live out an authentic faith, unbelievers will think they are judgmental people who merely follow religious rules. When churchgoers can't explain or defend their faith, it's no wonder why unbelievers think God doesn't exist, the Bible is a fairy tale, and Jesus Christ was "just a wise teacher" or a legend.

Ignoring God's Word is only one problem that nerfs you. However, it's a problem that makes you gullible and prone to sin, which nerfs you even more and opens the door for Satan to wreak havoc in your life and that of your family. He will attack your name — your character and integrity — in order to attack the name of Jesus Christ. Peter told us:

> *Be sober and self-controlled. Be watchful. Your adversary, the devil, walks around like a roaring lion, seeking whom he may devour.* (1 Peter 5:8 WEB)

And you should know the devil's roar doesn't necessarily sound like a lion's roar. Sometimes, it sounds like, "You seriously believe that Bible stuff?" "IF you ARE a Christian, how come you don't seem to know much?" An authentic Christian realizes his name — his character and integrity — is crucial. People recognized Joseph's, Daniel's, and Paul's character; people will recognize it in you when they see it. When your name shines, the name of Jesus Christ shines.

Maybe the things that come to mind when someone hears your name aren't so good — not even to your ears. There's no reason for that to remain so. Stop gaming around with your name and do something about it.

The first step is to de-nerf yourself. The fastest way to begin this process is to make intentional decisions to emerge from sin and ignorance of God's Word. I know people who resolved to listen to a Bible-in-a-year plan during their commutes. Others inconvenienced themselves by showing up earlier than usual for Sunday morning Bible studies or began attending a midweek small group. I know cohabitating couples who decided to get married and stopped sleeping together until after the ceremony. I have worked with men who are in the process of kicking pornography out of their lives. I know businessmen who have committed to leading their companies honestly and without exploiting their client's ignorance.

Little steps like starting Bible-reading plans, attending Bible studies, and praying can launch the transformation of your character and integrity.

As I mentioned earlier, Jesus' name means Yahweh Saves. His name is fitting since he is the way, the truth, and the life. No one comes to the Father except through him (John 14:6). Those are the facts no matter what Satan says, no matter what any atheist says, and no matter what "progressive" Christians say. The decisions you make to extract yourself from sin, bad relationships and situations, or to cure your ignorance about God and the Bible are all good. Still, they are not as foundational as the decision to place your faith and trust in Jesus as your Lord and Savior. Entering into a covenant with

God by confessing your faith in Jesus and being baptized opens the door for Jesus to enter your life and begin cleaning house.

DISCUSSION & REFLECTION

1. What is your honest evaluation of your name? In other words, are your character and integrity all that you'd like them to be?

2. Can you recognize ways you have been "nerfed" in the past year?

    ✗ Incidents that took the wind out of your sails?

    ✗ Decisions you made that turned out poorly?

    ✗ Sins or shortcomings that weakened you?

3. How have those incidents, decisions, or sins affected your relationship with God?

4. What two things can you start today to improve your character and integrity?

    ✗ _____

    ✗ _____

5. How do you think others perceive your character based on
   your actions and choices?

   ⚡ _____

6. What can you begin this week to actively address ignorance
   in your faith and equip yourself to deepen and defend your
   beliefs?

   ⚡ _____

   ⚡ _____

[4] Church Executive. https://churchexecutive.com/archives/church-trends-statistics-
[5] Ibid.

GAMING TRUTH

I read somewhere that our nation suffers from truth fatigue. Everybody has their own truth; no one knows what the truth is, and no one seems to be able to find the truth or get to the bottom of a matter. People who may or might not be telling the truth, who may or might not have ulterior motives, keep declaring, "This is the truth." It's frustrating at best. Nevertheless, we continue to pursue the truth. Well, sometimes.

The Bible tells us, *"The truth will set you free"* (John 8:32 NLT), but people who have never set foot in a church, who don't believe in the Bible, Jesus, or anything, love this little expression. I'll get to that.

REAL-TIME STRATEGY

In a Real-Time Strategy (RTS) game, you use strategy to build and create a society, system, kingdom, or situation that makes you happy and secure. If that sounds familiar to you, it's because that's what we do in real life all the time. We use strategy — some of us use more than others — to create a system that makes us happy. Maybe you want a system that helps you be financially secure, one with certain alliances that make you happy, or a kingdom that will enable you to withstand a government overthrow or survive the zombie apocalypse. We will strategize to build our empires according to our desires, which we believe will make us happy.

But how do you determine what will make you happy? This is an important question. How many celebrities have we heard say they thought they knew what they wanted, but it didn't bring the happiness they expected when they achieved it? That has probably happened to you.

> There is a way which seems right to a man, but its end is the way of death. (Proverbs 16:25 NASB)

When I was a child, I sometimes got up after everyone was asleep to watch late-night television. I loved a show called "Don Kirschner's Rock Concert" that showcased rock bands and artists performing live. I saw some great guitarists like Neal Schon, George Benson, and Al Di Meola doing their thing on stage. That was when I stopped wanting to be a doctor and started aspiring to be a rock star.

I took guitar lessons and practiced a lot. A lot! I played lead guitar in some cover bands in high school and dreamed of shredding in front of huge stadium crowds. Experiences in my little corner of the rock music world taught me two things. First, I rubbed elbows with some extraordinarily talented musicians who weren't making it. Not even close. Knowing they had skills many levels above mine humbled me, and I doubted I would achieve my dream. Second, most of the rock musicians in my circles were self-destructive types who were always conjuring up ways to blow up their lives. No offense to you rockers out there.

My point? I created a system I thought would make me happy. I poured my heart and soul into it only to discover I had been going full-throttle in the wrong direction.

Many of us discover such truth somewhere along the way. We made a wrong decision. Something we thought had been true all along turned out to be false. Or, like me, we found out we were going the wrong way.

This happens because we create our own "truth" by which we live — a way that seems right to us. Like an RTS, we build the system we want and then try to operate that way.

In John 18, we read about the Roman governor, Pontius Pilate, questioning Jesus. Jesus told Pilate his kingdom was not of this world.

> *Therefore, Pilate said to Him, "So You are a king?" Jesus answered, "You say correctly that I am a king. For this I have been born, and for this I have come into the world, to testify to the truth. Everyone who is of the truth hears My voice." Pilate said to Him, "What is truth?"* (John 18:37-38a NASB)

Earlier, I said everyone has their own truth, no one knows what the truth is, and no one ever seems to be able to find the truth or get to the bottom of a matter. That's where Pilate was. He found himself in a political triangle — his conscience bothered him concerning this Jesus, King of the Jews. He was convinced Jesus was innocent and certainly not worthy of crucifixion. Yet, he was responsible for calming the political tensions and rebellions in Israel or risk losing his position. He had to make himself look good to Rome.

TRUTH: WHAT WORKS OR WHAT YOU MAKE IT?

Maybe you wonder what truth is. Constantly speculating, never finding it, and often confused. Perhaps you question if the truth matters. Today, the most popular philosophy about truth is that "truth" is whatever works for you. We have a more-or-less RTS game society where "truth" is whatever you cling to, hoping it will make you happy. For some, truth is whatever they make it.

You hear this sort of thing all the time. "Just do whatever makes you happy," or "Live and let live," or "You do your thing and let others do theirs." It's practical and convenient — just going with the flow. An individual's "truth" is whatever their experience and perception of reality is. Popular daytime talk show hosts tout this philosophy.

The society you live in influences what you think about the world. Many in our culture suggest truth is like private property: it belongs to you, not someone else, much like your car belongs to you alone. Of course, if someone is living foolishly, that's their truth, and you can't tell anyone their truth isn't true.

It's a crazy, discouraging time to be alive, and relativizing truth like that significantly contributes to the turmoil in our present world. No one knows what the truth is; everyone thinks they have it; no one can find it, and you dare not tell anyone they're wrong.

But you understand this has nothing to do with the truth. Because what happens when what works for one person harms someone else? There are cultures where mutilating women is their way of life, and others where sexually abusing children is "normal." What worked for the Nazis was catastrophically horrible for everyone else. Can we really not discern what is true and what is false?

TRUTH CLAIM AS POWER GRAB

Since everyone is busy creating their own truth according to their desires and ambitions, you're not allowed to tell someone their truth isn't true. It's as if you're telling them they aren't allowed to have desires and ambitions.

So when you try to tell someone they're going the wrong way, they say you're making truth a power grab. Politicians do that all the time. They will make a truth claim, "My opponent is a scoundrel who just wants your votes. Vote for me!" Cults do this, too. "You are in the dark because you listen to other religious people. Listen to me, and you'll be enlightened!"

German philosopher Friedrich Nietzsche declared that people conceal unknown motives beneath their actions much like our skin covers our insides. He urged people to "squint maliciously" when someone would make a truth claim.[6] So whenever someone tells you, "You're wrong, listen to me," or, "This way is the right way," you may be suspicious about their motives, thinking (or squinting), "What is it you really want?"

Look at the situation Pilate was in.

> And they began to accuse Him, saying, "We found this man misleading our nation and forbidding to pay taxes to Caesar, and saying that He Himself is Christ, a King." (Luke 23:2 NASB)

Pilate listened to the accusations the Jewish leaders leveled at Jesus. Pilate questioned Jesus and rightly discerned Jesus was innocent.

> Then Pilate said to the chief priests and the crowds, "I find no guilt in this man." (Luke 23:4 NASB)

You see, Pilate was squinting — what do you really want?

But they kept on insisting, saying, "He stirs up the people, teaching all over Judea, starting from Galilee even as far as this place." (Luke 23:5 NASB)

Pilate was right to squint at the chief priests. They hated Jesus for exposing their hypocrisy, making them look bad, and threatening the system they had fabricated — a system they all profited from socially, politically, and financially. Their truth claims were false. They were manipulating Pilate so he would get rid of Jesus for them. Once Jesus was out of their way, those religious elites could continue their real-time strategy game. They would maintain the status quo in the system that benefited them. Sadly, Pilate did not stand by the truth and gave in to their false truth claims to retain his position of favor with both the Jews and the Romans.

The elites in control of our society say all truth claims are power grabs. That's part of the reason we see anarchy coming out of our higher education institutions. Some have pointed out that saying all truth claims are power grabs is itself a power grab.

The element of truth in all this is that most truth claims you hear are false. People throughout our society are gaming truth, creating their kingdoms according to their ambitions and desires, without regard to the harm caused to others. Even churchgoers do it. You'll hear people who go to church say things that are contrary to God's Word and God's way all the time.

"God wants you to be healthy and wealthy."

"Ahh, God doesn't care ...

" ... if we sleep around."

" ... that we live together."

" ... whether I get drunk or stay sober."

" ... whether I lie or tell the truth."

" ... whether you're anti-abortion or pro-abortion."

"God doesn't care what you do; he just loves and forgives; it's God's job."

Maybe you didn't know you were doing this, but making truth claims like those above is also a power grab. You are attempting to maintain control of your kingdom. You're trying to take control of God's Kingdom, too.

Some are reading this who, despite hearing the Gospel hundreds of times, fear that God might not love them and are afraid they'll be condemned. Others, too, although they are familiar with the Gospel, still believe they're "basically good" people who will get into heaven by doing more good things than bad things. They're all gaming truth — creating their own kingdoms according to their desires and ambitions and then believing that's the truth about God and their relationship with him. In doing so, they present a warped version of Christianity to the world.

Look at what Paul wrote in Romans chapter 1.

> For the wrath of God is revealed from heaven against all ungodliness and unrighteousness of men who suppress the truth in unrighteousness. (Romans 1:18 WEB)

We need to come to terms with the fact that churchgoers sometimes suppress the truth with their unrighteousness. How so? When you sin, you behave according to the worldly ambitions and desires of the kingdom you created instead of behaving according to God's Kingdom and desires. When a churchgoer does this, he expresses a truth claim that is contrary to God's truth.

You see this happen everywhere. You even do it yourself because our desires are arbitrary — they frequently change like feelings. One day, you feel very close to God, but you feel very distant the next day. Feelings and desires can be irrational.

Maybe you had a bad day at work and suddenly feel like you want to quit, like God doesn't love you, and like nothing's working out. And when you don't feel good, you'll be tempted to pay attention to all the false truth claims people fling everywhere. Our faulty thinking and false truth claims keep us weak, doubting, and completely self-absorbed.

John Njoroge is a theologian and scholar from Kenya. When he attended his mother's funeral, family and friends expected him to say some words since they considered him the family's best-educated and most mature Christian. But when the time came, he just couldn't. He recounted that his feelings were so intense and his grief so deep that he couldn't make sense of his mother's untimely death. In those moments, he realized he could never depend on his feelings. There will be times when you have to rely on the truth you know.

But how do you know the truth? People love to throw around the expression, "The truth will set you free," and they use it to justify their truth claims and power grabs. They have torn this wonderful expression out of context and have changed its meaning — gaming truth — to suit their desires. You ought to learn what the expression means because just knowing a celebrity's view of "truth" will not set you free.

So Jesus said to the Jews who had believed
in him, "If you abide in my word, you are
truly my disciples, and you will know the
truth, and the truth will set you free." (John
8:31-32 ESV)

And there we have it: the truth that will set you free is God's Word. You must abide in it. That means you know it, love it, obey it, and make it your life source. Then you will know the truth, and the truth will set you free.

The Bible teaches us the truth about our origin — we were not an accident of the cosmos — we were created to rule under his dominion, enjoy fellowship with God, and help creation flourish (Genesis 1:28). The Bible teaches us the truth about sin and our fallen nature — our sins put a wall between us and God (Isaiah 59:2). The Bible says we are not "basically good" people; all have sinned and fall short of God's glory; we are sinners who have rebelled against God, our Creator, and stand under judgment (Psalms 14 and 53, Romans 3).

But because of God's great love for us, the Bible teaches us the truth about God's overarching plan of redemption to save humankind from the ultimate penalty of sin. God himself became flesh and dwelt among us — Jesus Christ, the embodiment of truth (John 1). He lived the obedient life we were expected to live and died the death we should have suffered in order to satisfy God's holy and righteous requirements for our salvation (Romans 3, 2 Corinthians 5, Hebrews 2).

Jesus' one act of righteousness brings us into a right relationship with God and new life for everyone (Romans 3:21-26). The Bible teaches us the truth about how to belong to him: by turning away from the false truth claims we've adhered to and surrendering to him to be reconciled to God and adopted into his family (Acts 2, Romans 3 and 6).

The Bible teaches us the truth about our ultimate destiny:

> *He who overcomes will inherit these things, and I will be his God and he will be My son. But for the cowardly and unbelieving and abominable and murderers and immoral persons and sorcerers and idolaters and all liars, their part will be in the lake that burns with fire and brimstone, which is the second death.* (Revelation 21:7-8 NASB)

These truths may be sobering, but they also encourage us. They draw us deeper into God and his Word, less deeply into ourselves, and thus more apt to see this world's truth claims for what they are — power grabs. The enemy cunningly uses the world's truth claims to distract us from the truth of God and his Son, Jesus Christ, and that was Pilate's struggle.

> *Therefore, Pilate said to Him, "So You are a king?" Jesus answered, "You say correctly that I am a king. For this I have been born, and for this I have come into the world, to testify to the truth. Everyone who is of the truth hears My voice." Pilate said to Him, "What is truth?"* (John 18:37-38a NASB)

I imagine Pilate had more than his fill of false truth claims while governor in Israel. Jesus told him he came to bear witness to the truth. Pilate looked truth in the face, quipped, **"What is truth?"** and left.

> *And when he had said this, he went out again to the Jews and said to them, "I find no guilt in Him. But you have a custom that I release someone for you at the Passover; do you wish then that I release for you the King of the Jews?" So they cried out again, saying, "Not this Man, but Barabbas." Now Barabbas was a robber.* (John 18:38b-40 NASB)

Pilate was so tired of the truth games and power grabs that he condemned the truth and acquitted the robber. We do the same when we pay attention to false truth claims people fling around — we are gaming the truth. The university professor says, "There is no God." Popular talk show hosts say, "All paths lead to god." But Jesus said:

> *I am the way, and the truth, and the life. No one comes to the Father except through me.*
> (John 14:6 ESV)

People like to play their own real-time strategy games. They'll use their skills and resources to build systems according to their desires and ambitions. Rusty will create his kingdom to make himself feel happy and secure. But Rusty will inevitably find that something he thought had been true was false. He'll realize he had been going the wrong way all along. It didn't bring the happiness he expected, and he discovered he had been gaming the truth.

> *There is a way which seems right to a man, but its end is the way of death.* (Proverbs 16:25 NASB)

If you cling to your own ideas of what the truth is like instead of abiding in God's truth, then you're rejecting Jesus and have invited Barabbas into your life instead. What was he? A robber. And that's what gaming the truth does — it robs you of the real truth: the truth that sets you free.

DISCUSSION & REFLECTION

1. Describe a time you realized you were going in the wrong direction.

     ✗ What did you do to correct your course? Or —

     ✗ What should you have done?

2. Describe a situation where you recognized someone was making a truth claim as a power grab.

     ✗ What did you do?

     ✗ Did you feel manipulated?

     ✗ When Jesus presents his truth claims, do you get the impression he is making a power grab? Why or why not?

3. People and organizations can sometimes steer you down a pathway because they want something from you.

     ✗ List two robbers in your life, past or present.

     ✗ _____

     ✗ _____

⚡ What have you done (or what can you do) to halt those robbers and get yourself back on better footing?

⚡ _____

⚡ _____

4. How do you ensure your faith is authentic and not merely a product of societal influences or personal desires?

5. What practices or habits can help you stay grounded in God's truth?

6. In what areas of your life do you sometimes succumb to false beliefs or societal pressures?

⚡ _____

⚡ _____

⚡ What verses or passages could you memorize to better resist them?

⚡ _____

⚡ _____

7. What biblical truth has challenged your worldview or perspectives the most?

_____ Chapter 3 Notes

[6] Merold Westphal, Suspicion & Faith: The Religious Uses of Modern Atheism (Grand Rapids: William B. Eerdmans Publishing Company, 1993), 220-221.

GAMING THE INSTRUCTIONS

Even though I use gaming terms to springboard into discipleship topics in this book, I do not consider living the Christian life a game. In fact, I hope the gaming terminology helps us recognize that many of us churchgoers are indeed playing games with life, faith, church, and so on.

So, if you bought a game system and an interesting-looking game, how would you learn how to play it? We often learn the ropes of a new game by having someone initiate us. Typically, a friend or online video shows you some of the basics of the game in just a few minutes.

OR! Maybe you could read the instructions! If you're a dad, I'm sure you're cringing right now. But listen, I've bought enough of those "unfun" toys for our kids that said "some assembly required" on the box (and always had leftover parts) to know that it's good to read the instructions.

XP

You don't need to read much about a role-playing game to learn the basics. Once you know a few fundamentals, you can begin developing your skills and strategies. You will quickly start accumulating Experience Points (XP).

When you start playing a game, you're not skilled: you don't have much XP yet. But as you play a game, advancing through the levels, learning the backstory, and reaching benchmarks, you gain experience points.

BUFF

The more XP you gain, the more buffs (positive effects) you get. Your farm becomes more profitable, your space station gains extra defense, or your power, weapons, and abilities improve.

While accumulating XP and buffs may lead to better outcomes in the game, there is much more to your progress than the stats you've achieved through hours of grinding. Even if you're well-versed in the fundamentals, thriving in the game requires a deeper level of skill and strategic thinking.

SCRUB

The journey to becoming an adept player is not without its pitfalls. Many players who don't put in the work to improve will still have an inflated ego and will tend to blame hacking or cheesing for their defeats. We affectionately refer to these players as scrubs.

DLC

Whether you're an adept player, a novice, or a straight-up scrub, nothing takes the gameplay experience to the next level like Downloadable Content (DLC). This may include weapons or character skins, new plots and quests, or even exclusive gear. DLC opens up game features that were previously inaccessible to the player.

My family and I served as Bible Translators in Africa among a Bible-less people. Once, while walking in our neighborhood, we saw some kids throwing rocks at a chameleon. On another occasion, we saw kids beating a puppy with sticks. The puppy didn't do anything wrong; he was just in the wrong place at the wrong time.

But these kids never got the DLC that you and I take for granted — things we draw from the Bible. Ideas like, "God made the puppy; God loves the puppy." And ideas like, "God made you; God loves you."

This chapter is entitled Gaming the Instructions, and the "instructions" refer to God's Word: the Bible. Some think of the Bible as our instruction manual because it's where we learn basic truths like "God made me; God loves me."

I want to take a look at a verse from Hebrews chapter 4. Before focusing on that verse, which talks about the Word of God, we need to understand the context. When the author of the book of Hebrews mentions God's Word here, he's wrapping up an argument he began in chapter 3: the people whom Moses led out of Egypt refused to believe God's Word and obey God's Word. Therefore, God declared they would not enter his rest.

Then he says we, who follow Jesus Christ, face the same alternatives of rest or wrath. He urges his readers not to reject God's Word or refuse to believe it.

Then he wrote:

> For the word of God is living and active and sharper than any two-edged sword, and piercing as far as the division of soul and spirit, of both joints and marrow, and able to judge the thoughts and intentions of the heart. (Hebrews 4:12 NASB)

Now that we understand Hebrews 4:12 in its context, I want to look at what this verse tells us about God's instructions.

GOD'S WORD IS LIVING AND ACTIVE

It's become cliché to say it, but the Bible IS unlike any other book — it lays the claim that it is living and active. The way it is written in Greek as a present active participle tells us it is alive and working. The word translated as "active" means it is effective; it can get it done. That's why some of your translations say "powerful." No other book on the face of the earth has continued for millennia throughout history to actively transform people.

I heard of one guy whose pastor told him he should read God's Word. The man said, "I've gone through the Bible several times, but I've received no inspiration at all from it." The elderly pastor replied, "Hmm. Maybe you should try letting it, for once, go through you, then you will tell a very different story."

You see, this guy had gone through the motions of grinding through the Bible, but despite having some XP, he became a scrub and blamed the Bible for his own shortcomings.

I have an African friend named Sonny.[7] He was a drunk, a wife-beater, a child-cusser-outer, etc.

When a colleague of mine began translating the Bible in Sonny's village, Sonny heard God's Word preached in his own language for the first time. And God's Word transformed Sonny.

Since then, Sonny has become one of the godliest men in his village. His wife is happy, joyful, and proud of him, and his children adore him. His entire village knows they can count on his justice, honesty, and family advice. Some villagers have even asked him to raise their kids! Sonny and his family are among the few Christians in an area dominated by a different world religion, yet many have decided to follow Jesus Christ because of Sonny.

Sonny went through a dramatic transformation that affected every aspect of his life. God's Word opened up a whole new world of features and truths that were previously inaccessible to Sonny and others in his village — ideas like, "God made the puppy; God loves the puppy," and, "God made you; God loves you."

Sonny was given access to God's DLC, and it gave him a whole new life and a whole new quest. Praise God his Word is living and active. Get into it, and let it get into you.

GOD'S WORD IS SHARP AND PIERCING

Hebrews 4:12 also tells us God's Word is:

> ... *sharper than any two-edged sword, and*
> *piercing as far as the division of soul and*
> *spirit, of both joints and marrow.* (Hebrews
> 4:12 NASB)

The Romans used two swords; one was a large, broad sword called a Spatha[8] they would use in war. The other was a smaller two-edged sword called, in Latin, a Gladius.[9] The Greek word the author of Hebrews used, however, is Machaira. It is a general term for sword, similar in size to the Gladius, but described as "a single-edged slashing weapon with a curved blade."[10] Outside the context of combat, the word is also used to refer to "a surgeon's scalpel."[11] This is why I find this word choice so amazing.

Some people use the Bible as a weapon and beat others with it. I'm not convinced that is the way God's Word works. I've also known plenty of people who think you're beating them over the head with the Bible just by mentioning it. But the Word of God is sharp and piercing when it gets into you, not when you try to bash someone else with it.

Hebrews 4 isn't talking about how you use God's Word on others; it shows how God uses his Word in you. God's Word illuminates (Psalm 119:105), rebukes, corrects, and trains (2 Timothy 3:15-17), and is the primary source of wisdom and truth (John 8:31-32, Psalm 119:130). When you get God's Word in you, you experience its transforming power to affirm your value in the Kingdom, but also to convict you of your sin. Jesus uses it like a scalpel to cut away the sin, pain, and corruption that keep you sick.

GOD'S WORD IS DISCERNING

Finally, Hebrews 4:12 tells us God's Word is discerning; it says it:

> ... *is able to discern the thoughts and intentions of the heart.* (Hebrews 4:12 WEB)

Some of your translations say it "judges." That's fine; both are valid translations of "kritikos," the Greek word from which we get our English word "critic." This is what God's Word does in us — it passes judgment on our thoughts and motives.

One reason so many people are offended by the Bible is that some Christians use God's Word in an offensive way — to pierce others, to judge others. But the main reason people are offended by the Bible (and it's the same reason you are sometimes offended by the Bible) is that it's offensive! It makes you uncomfortable when you aren't walking in truth.

God's Word is living and active. It is indeed sharp, piercing, and judging, too. It pokes you. It is meant to convict you of your sin. The Apostle James wrote:

> Draw near to God and He will draw near to you. Cleanse your hands, you sinners; and purify your hearts, you double-minded. (James 4:8 NASB)

Nobody likes being called a double-minded sinner. It makes us uncomfortable. God's Word does that intentionally because, as long as we're comfortable, we won't address the things in us that need to change.

God's Word prods you. Matthew records an account of Jesus rebuking the Pharisees in Matthew 23. Jesus told them they were obeying little insignificant rules but failing to obey the most essential elements of the Law. Then, he added:

> ... but these are the things you should have done without neglecting the others. (Matthew 23:23 NASB)

Jesus made it clear that you mustn't pick and choose the parts of God's Word you like and discard the rest. That is gaming the instructions.

God's Word enlightens you. In the renowned Sermon on the Mount, Jesus said:

> *For where your treasure is, there your heart*
> *will be also.* (Matthew 6:21 NASB)

God's Word makes it clear to us that the things we lust after distract us from God and his Word, keep us nerfed, and cause us to remain scrubs and uninterested in God's downloadable content. We may feel content with believing in God without needing to study his Word or follow the instructions.

The Apostle James wrote:

> *You believe that God is one; you do well.*
> *Even the demons believe—and shudder!*
> (James 2:19 ESV)

Satan and his demons all know the basics just as well as the typical churchgoer — better, even! Knowing the basics can be enough to begin your relationship with Jesus Christ, but the last thing you want to do is remain an immature baby Christian.

You would never tolerate a role-playing game where you remained stuck on the first level or two like an eternal scrub. Of course not! You want to develop skills, enhance your strategies, get exclusive late-game features, and advance to higher levels and tiers.

It's the same with your relationship with Jesus Christ. If you learned the basics to "get saved" but are not regularly in God's

Word, chances are you are a scrub. You're unskilled concerning your life in Christ while thinking you're fine. But as soon as a setback happens — you get laid off, or tragedy strikes — you discover just how unskilled you are. You become confused and don't know how to face it. That's what happens when we game the instructions. Gaming the instructions doesn't work in any other area of life either. Maybe you think you know all you need to know about God's Word, but —

Remember when you tried to put those Ikea dining chairs together without the instructions? And the crib? You unwittingly assembled a trebuchet catapult for your baby — and isn't that embarrassing!

God's Word is the downloadable content we need. We need God's instruction. Each of us has too many sharp edges for God's Word to not be sharp and piercing — we need to be smoothed out. Some of us do not welcome this news, and you know why. Everyone wants their way, and no one wants to be uncomfortable.

We beg God to see us and turn his attention toward us when we are hurting, threatened, or at the end of our rope. But we'd really like him to look the other way regarding our shortcomings and sins. God doesn't do that because he knows our sin is a cancer that eats away at us. Without his sharp, piercing, discerning Word, our sin-cancer would ruin us. We need the transformation his Word does in us.

I hope you go through God's Word. When you do, my prayer is that you let it go through you. Be offended, be humbled, but be transformed by the living and active, sharp and piercing Word of God Almighty.

> *Trust in Yahweh with all your heart, and don't lean on your own understanding. In all your ways acknowledge him, and he will make your paths straight.* (Proverbs 3:5-6 WEB)

Learning the basics and having a little XP are not enough for you to thrive or get buffed. Many churchgoers know the basics and appear to have their XP but continue to be scrubs.

You need downloadable content. Just like you can get exclusive features in a role-playing game by downloading those extras, you get exclusive features like wisdom, understanding, spiritual and practical insights, and discernment from the downloadable content in God's Word. You can get that DLC with your printed Bible, but other ways exist today.

You can download the YouVersion Bible app[12] on your phone, tablet, or computer. If you do, you can listen to God's Word — whatever language and translation you prefer — as your device reads the Bible aloud to you. The app boasts thousands of Bible reading plans — read through the entire Bible, just one book, or just a few. Many plans include devotionals that explain passages, and some have extraordinarily creative videos.

I urge you to get involved in a small group where they go through God's Word in person. Nowadays, many Bible studies are video-driven and have books to follow along. Whatever you do, make the effort to be intentional about encountering God's Word in a way that reveals its complexities, relevance, and power in our lives.

Everyone has challenges, issues, and blind spots that need God's attention. Time in the Word of God is a fantastic way to shine light on those and add some healing salt. At the same time, everyone has strengths, experiences, and other resources they can contribute in a group Bible study setting. This enables each person to speak into the lives of the other members.

I was one of the most pathetic and lost souls ever until God began transforming me from the inside out. God's Word was the principal way God did that. So don't game the instructions. The Bible serves us as a divine compass. It gives clear, reliable directions and has survived and thrived for millennia. It continues to transform the lost into the saved, wrongdoers into men and women of honor, and God-haters into missionaries.

On the other hand, the world transforms no one for the better — it doesn't love you, doesn't forgive you, and makes you like an aimless wave blown here and there by every changing wind (Ephesians 4:14, James 1:6). A secular worldview is like a compass that cannot recognize true north — no way can you trust the directions you get from the world.

Remember, it's not enough to own an instruction manual. You have to get into God's Word and let it get into you to have its transforming effect. It's my prayer you do just that.

DISCUSSION & REFLECTION

1. Which of the following statements describes best how you currently feel about the Bible?

    a. I'm not interested in the Bible because

    _____.

    b. I know a lot about the Bible, but I'm not very good at living by it.

    c. When I read the Bible, I have a hard time understanding it.

    d. The Bible really transformed me, and I enjoy reading it.

    NOTE: If you selected a, b, or c, and someone else in your group chose d, ask them for ideas to up your game with some DLC.

2. Describe a time when the Bible felt sharp and piercing to you.

   ⚔ Do you still have difficulty with that issue?

   ⚔ If so, ask others in your group who may be buffs to speak into your life on that issue.

   ⚔ How does such discomfort bring about change in us?

3. James 2:19 explicitly says evil spirits know God exists and that He is one. Nevertheless, they do not love, follow, or worship God.

   ⚔ What sets you apart from such evil spirits?

   ⚔ _____

4. Can you recognize ways the world or a secular worldview has nerfed you and made you a scrub?

   ⚔ _____

   ⚔ _____

   ⚔ _____

Chapter 4 Notes

[7] Not his real name.
[8] https://worldhistory.us/ancient-history/ancient-rome/swords-of-the-roman-empire.php
[9] https://historycooperative.org/roman-weapons/
[10] https://ralspaugh.wordpress.com/2019/07/01/biblical-weaponry/
[11] https://www.comitatus.net/greekswords.html
[12] https://www.youversion.com/the-bible-app/

CHAPTER FIVE

GAMING THE BOSS

In role-playing games, a Boss is an enemy you meet at the end of a level. The boss is more powerful than the other enemies you have encountered, and overcoming him will take extra forethought, strategy, and skill.

The boss isn't your only opponent in role-playing games. You might be up against computer villains or other gamers. Either way, you usually play against an opponent on the same tier: the ranking level you are on. In multiplayer games, players of similar experience levels (XP) are matched up to keep things fair. That way, highly experienced veterans aren't demoralizing beginners.

OWNED & GANKED

However, you may sometimes play against another gamer who is way out of your league. You will likely get creamed if your opponent has a great XP advantage. When you're easily beaten in a game, players may say you've been "owned" or "pwned."[13] It is no fun being owned, of course, but many gamers love to annihilate a less-experienced noob.

In such a case, when the player with the overwhelming XP advantage obliterates you, players will say he ganked you. Matchmaking in online games isn't always balanced. "Smurfs" are buffs and scrubs who will create low-level accounts so they can gank low-level players. These "masters in noob's clothing" are common. They love to dominate, ambush, and humiliate players with less XP.

People get owned and ganked all the time in real life. Supervisors take credit for all the department's successes but then blame the subordinates when there's a failure. Or the insurance refuses to pay your claim. You might sometimes feel like a grade-schooler taking on a sumo wrestler.

A good verse to keep in mind is 1 John 4:4.

> *You are from God, little children, and have*
> *overcome them; because greater is He who is*
> *in you than he who is in the world.* (1 John
> 4:4 NASB)

I cannot overstate how important it is to understand this verse. John is talking about having overcome the enemies of the Gospel. He groups false teachers, false prophets, and false teachings and philosophies all together, and he refers to them as **"the spirit of the antichrist"** (1 John 4:3 NASB). The Apostle John isn't giving us reason to be arrogant or obnoxious, but he reveals a critical truth here. Let me explain it this way.

In Acts chapter 3, we read the account of when Peter and John went to the temple for the afternoon prayers. They saw a lame man sitting and begging for alms at one of the temple gates. If you grew up going to children's Sunday school, the song might already be playing in your head.

> *But Peter said, "I do not possess silver and*
> *gold, but what I do have I give to you: In the*
> *name of Jesus Christ the Nazarene-*
> *walk!"* (Acts 3:6 NASB)

At that, the lame man stood up, entered the temple courts, and began leaping and jumping with joy. Everyone gathered around, amazed at the miracle that was performed. And Peter proclaimed to them that they (Peter and John) did not make this man well, but Jesus Christ worked through their faith to heal this lame man. Peter gave them the Good News — how Jesus is the fulfillment of God's promise to Abraham to bless all the peoples of the earth, the fulfillment of all the prophets had spoken, and how he was resurrected from the dead to prove it (Acts 3:7-26).

That was when a group of priests and other leaders arrived on the scene and arrested them for teaching about Jesus at the temple. The religious elites jailed Peter and John overnight, and the high priest and the Council of leaders interrogated them the next day.

> Then Peter, filled with the Holy Spirit, said to them, "Rulers of the people and elders, if we are being examined today concerning a good deed done to a crippled man, by what means this man has been healed, let it be known to all of you and to all the people of Israel that by the name of Jesus Christ of Nazareth, whom you crucified, whom God raised from the dead—by him this man is standing before you well. This Jesus is the stone that was rejected by you, the builders, which has become the cornerstone. And

> *there is salvation in no one else, for there is*
> *no other name under heaven given among*
> *men by which we must be saved." Now*
> *when they saw the boldness of Peter and*
> *John, and perceived that they were unedu-*
> *cated, common men, they were astonished.*
> *And they recognized that they had been*
> *with Jesus.* (Acts 4:8-13 ESV)

The high priest, scribes, and elders of the powerful Sanhedrin council were there. These men were top-tier grandmasters who knew every in and out of the system. They had serious social clout, political power, intellectual ammo, and financial means. These elites surrounded Peter and John, two uneducated fishermen grunts from backwater Galilee County. This was an opportunity for some major-league pwning. Yet, the Jewish leaders merely scolded Peter and John, commanding them not to teach anymore about Jesus. Peter and John rejected that in front of everyone present. Nevertheless, the Council released them.

What could explain Peter and John's boldness in the face of such intimidating odds against them? We find the answer to that question in what happened after they reunited with their Christian brothers and sisters. They prayed. It's a fantastic prayer, and I hope you'll read it later. You will find the whole account in Acts chapters 3 and 4. But here is a particular point in what they prayed:

> *And now, Lord, look upon their threats and grant to your servants to continue to speak your word with all boldness.* (Acts 4:29 ESV)

What's the first thing we pray when we face a difficult situation? "Oh Lord, take this problem away." "Oh Lord, give us relief." "Oh Lord, help me not be in these circumstances." "Oh Lord, help this never to happen again!"

But Peter and John did not pray that way. They prayed that the Lord would help them remain bold as they spoke the truth about him. They knew the One who was in them was greater than those who were in the world. They knew they didn't heal the lame man — Jesus did. They knew they had no power whatsoever in and of themselves. Where did they get their power?

It was Jesus who worked through their faith in him. Even when the high priest and the Council antagonized them, Peter was filled with the Holy Spirit. They relied on God's power, not their own human power.

Paul understood this, too. He wrote two letters to Timothy, a young church planter he trained. In 2 Timothy chapter one, he told Timothy:

For God did not give us a Spirit of fear but of power and love and self-control. (2 Timothy 1:7 NET)

Whenever I read this verse, and others like it, I think of unbelievers who try to pwn believers by saying, "It's fine to worship in a church building or in the privacy of your home but leave your faith out of every other area of life."

They don't fully understand who Jesus Christ is. Or what it's like to know the Creator of heaven and earth loves you. Or what it's like to know you are so precious to him that he would go to the cross in your place to reconcile and redeem you. Or what it's like to know your purpose, the meaning of life, and your glorious destiny. They don't understand what it's like to have the Holy Spirit in them. They are, instead, guided by the spirit of the deceiver who opposes the truth. That's why they insist you leave your faith within the walls of a building! Don't fall for it!

Even progressive Christians can echo the secular view of practicing one's faith only in private. But true believers know that authentic faith impacts every aspect of life. Faith in Jesus transforms you from the inside out and affects your beliefs as well as your behavior, no matter where you are. It demands a radical change in worldview that is counter-cultural.

TANKS

In role-based (or class-based) games, an ideal team will include at least one Tank — a character who can take a lot of punishment without weakening or dying. The role of a tank is to draw fire away from other "squishy" characters who would otherwise get easily pwned.

When times are good and things are going well, any churchgoer can be in a good mood and have a positive outlook. However, you know this: many churchgoers slump when times take a turn and things aren't going well. But not the tanks. Not much gets to them. Their health levels remain high when hard times come, and they keep trucking forward.

Know any Christian tanks? They are gifted with resilience. They're able to stand firm in their faith and provide stability during challenging times. They take on heavier burdens and create a strong foundation for the group. They tend to have stellar integrity and to be well-rooted in biblical truth. No matter what happens, they always remain even-keel; they don't let much bother them. These types of Christians often surprise you with just how resilient they are. Nothing gets them down. What's their secret? It's who they know, what they know, and what's in them.

WHO THEY KNOW

First and foremost, they *know* Jesus Christ — they don't merely know *about* him. Christian tanks are those who signed on with Jesus but not just for fire insurance. They understand the truth of who Jesus Christ is; they know the Creator of heaven and earth loves them and considers them so precious that he went to the cross in their place. They have clung to Jesus through many difficult times and learned from those experiences that a daily walk with the Lord and a steady diet of prayer and time in God's Word strengthen their faith.

You may know some Christians who are tanks. They have become quite resilient by putting what they know of Jesus to the test and witnessing God bring them through many challenges. Their experiences and knowledge of Jesus enable them to face things differently than your average churchgoer.

Speaking of facing things.

I have come alongside and counseled many churchgoers who can't seem to get past cravings, addictions, failure, and guilt. I'm not saying overcoming is easy. They may make a little progress but then get ganked by the same old enemies. If this describes you, one helpful solution is to spend more time with tanks. You probably know a Christian or two at church or work who is unshakable and resilient. Spend more time with them and learn from them.

SUPPORTS

Not all teammates will be tanks. Tanks work alongside other players so that the team can move toward the goal. Support characters have a range of abilities to heal and buff their teammates to keep them alive and effective. They come alongside others, offering the advantages they bring to the team.

Imagine you and your allies are facing a boss in an RPG. Your tank runs up front to take the brunt of the boss's attacks, but the whole team is still losing health (especially the tank). The boss is debuffing your team to the point that they can hardly make any progress. That's when your support player comes in, replenishes everyone's health, and adds buffs to your characters, making them faster, stronger, and more effective despite the enemy's schemes. Supports may not always be on the front lines and may not see half as much action as the tank, but they are instrumental in helping the party stand strong against the boss's onslaught.

In a church community, supports offer encouragement, comfort, and assistance. They lift others up in prayer and discern what kind of help a brother or sister needs. Supports may or might not be tanks themselves. Still, by applying their gifts, skills, and advantages to the benefit of their church community, they help churchgoers become more resilient — more tanky.

DPS

Revisiting our RPG scenario, your team is doing well with resilient tanks and revitalizing supports, but the last key ingredient you need to thwart the enemy's schemes is a DPS.

DPS, "Damage-Per-Second" characters, are the "swords" of the team. They are hard-wired to inflict concentrated damage and score the maximum number of kills per round. Your tanks and supports might be able to hold their own against a boss or a horde of enemies, but when your DPS comes in, they arrive with an arsenal of weapons specialized to break down the enemy's defenses, kill minions with one hit, and bring the bosses to their knees.

Likewise, DPS characters in the church community are hard-wired with a knack for knowing God's Word — *"the sword of the Spirit"* (Ephesians 6:17) — and discernment for how to apply it. These believers get involved in exhorting and discipling others and actively engage in intercessory prayer.

However, in both RPGs and church communities, the most consistent downfall of a DPS is isolation. There are countless DPS characters who are notorious for never sticking with their team and solely relying on their own abilities without cover or support. Try to guess who gets ganked the most!

> *Two are better than one because they have a good return for their labor. For if either of them falls, the one will lift up his companion. But woe to the one who falls when there is not another to lift him up.* (Ecclesiastes 4:9-10 NASB)

WINGMEN

I encourage every man to get a *wingman:* someone he trusts and who has the courage to tell him truths he might not want to hear. Every Christian hoping to thrive in his faith would do well to surround himself with tanks, supports, and DPSs, and stick with them for stability, encouragement, and exhortation.

Supports and DPSs tend to be squishier and need tanks to lean on. DPSs and tanks will eventually get worn down and pwned if they don't have the proper support. Tanks and supports need DPSs to back them with firepower so they can press forward. Tanks, DPSs, and supports all need one another, and I believe Paul the Apostle would agree based on what he wrote in 1 Corinthians chapter 12.

Motivational speaker Jim Rohn is credited with this fantastic modern proverb:

> **"You are the average of the five people you spend the most time with."**

If your inner circle consists of scrubs, meaning you always hang out with people of your same or lesser caliber or who struggle with the same cravings, addictions, and shortcomings as you do, you will live a nerfed life.

In Chapter 3, I mentioned that I played guitar in several rock bands when I was in high school. I poured all my time, energy, and money into becoming a rock star, squandering my grades and reputation to follow that dream. A few experiences showed me (1) I didn't have the transcendent skill required, and (2) most of the rock musicians I rubbed elbows with were swirling down the toilet and looking for someone else's heel to grab on their way.

In the modern world, the number of people swirling down the toilet has grown exponentially — more people than ever are looking to grab your heel and drag you down the chute with them. Finding good wingmen (tanks, DPSs, and supports) is more crucial than ever now. Finding a healthy church in this modern age is getting more challenging, but that is the first and easiest place to look for such wingmen.

Having a good wingman is beneficial, if not crucial, for getting past challenges, overcoming hordes of enemies, and advancing to the next level. All this will help you gain XP and strengthen your faith.

WHAT THEY KNOW

These resilient Christians, such as tanks, DPSs, and supports, who we look to as our wingmen, didn't start out steadfast in faith, and neither do we. Yes, they sought Jesus, came to know Jesus, and had wingmen in their lives to learn from as they began living out their faith. But we all need more if we hope to mature and become resilient. After all, little children need their parents all the time initially. But as they get older, children don't mature well if their parents hover over them all the time. In addition to what we learn from our wingmen, we need to learn from God's Word.

Any tank can tell you that what they know from the Bible affirms their faith and identity, informs their walk and behavior, and strengthens them to meet the challenges of life in a dark world. Look how David draws his strength from the DLC of God's Word:

> *In God, I will praise his word. In Yahweh, I will praise his word. I have put my trust in God. I will not be afraid. What can man do to me?* (Psalm 56:10-11 WEB)

If you think you have to be a self-sufficient super-Christian to have such confident trust, then you may have set yourself up to be ganked. In video games, you have to face different enemies. You have a boss to go up against at the end of the level before advancing to the next one. Without incorporating God's Word into their faith walk, most churchgoers don't have what it takes to make it past the boss's minions, much less conquer the boss.

> *But now Yahweh who created you, Jacob, and he who formed you, Israel says: "Don't be afraid, for I have redeemed you. I have called you by your name. You are mine. When you pass through the waters, I will be with you; and through the rivers, they will not overflow you. When you walk through the fire, you will not be burned, and flame will not scorch you. For I am Yahweh your God, the Holy One of Israel, your Savior. ...* (Isaiah 43:1-3a WEB)

Isaiah specified "when" you pass through waters, not "if." And "when" you walk through the fire, not "if." Much like you face obstacles in your RPGs, you will pass through some waters and have to walk through some fire in real life. It's crucial to know that each of us will suffer and experience lows. The rain of tragedy and trials falls on everyone. What will you do when those hard times come? Get mad at God?

Maybe you'll feel like the writer of Psalm 73, where he says:

> *All in vain have I kept my heart clean and washed my hands in innocence.* (Psalm 73:13 ESV)

In modern vernacular, he's saying, "Look at all the good things I've done, yet God hasn't made things go my way!" Pay attention. If you're struggling, suffering, or feeling like you're continually getting owned, it is not time to shrink back. It's time to look at how the enemy is trying to distract you from drawing on the strength of God — that is the enemy's strategy. It's time to mobilize your wingmen, upgrade your DLC, and lean more on the Lord who is in you and is greater than he who is in the world (1 John 4:4). It's time for more Jesus Christ in your life, not less. That will transform you from someone who is routinely ganked into someone as resilient as a tank, as encouraging as a support, and as discerning as a DPS.

In Ephesians chapter 6, Paul wrote this:

> *Finally, be strong in the Lord, and in the strength of his might. Put on the whole armor of God, that you may be able to stand against the wiles of the devil. For our wrestling is not against flesh and blood, but against the principalities, against the powers, against the world's rulers of the darkness of this age, and against the spiritual forces of wickedness in the heavenly places.* (Ephesians 6:10-12 WEB)

Paul is telling us this life isn't fair. You're up against forces you can't see, against powers in a realm — the spiritual realm — which can gank you in a heartbeat.

So he tells us:

> *Therefore put on the whole armor of God, that you may be able to withstand in the evil day, and, having done all, to stand.* (Ephesians 6:13 WEB)

Your armor? **Your** XP? **Your** skills and strategies? Alone, they do very little for you. Take up God's armor, not your own.

> *Stand therefore, having the utility belt of truth buckled around your waist, and having put on the breastplate of righteousness,* (Ephesians 6:14 WEB)

What truth? **Your** truth? The **world's** truth? No! Only God's truth is unchangeable and inherently good and right — you can trust it. Paul described it as a belt — God's truth gives you support and holds everything together. The fact that we are to "stand" with God's truth tells us we must possess it, and then we can depend on it when we go up against forces of evil.

And what righteousness? Your own? No! God's righteousness. There is an ethical side to righteousness: moral principles and standards. You are to pattern your speech and behavior so that justice, peace, and good prevail. But here, Paul described righteousness as a breastplate (a protective piece of armor), so he is not saying that your morality is the breastplate. He is referring to the righteousness that God bestows on you when you place your faith and trust in him and enter into a covenant with him. How does that protect you? The righteousness of Christ guards your **identity** in him. Satan, demons, and unbelievers like to point out how imperfect you are. They have a point. You fall short. We all do. But whoever you used to be is history. Because you have placed your faith and trust in him, he has bestowed his righteousness on you — you have a new identity as his child with all the rights, privileges, and responsibilities of a son. Again, this is what tanks, DPSs, and supports know — knowing this is part of what makes them healthy, steadfast, and courageous.

> *and having fitted your feet with the preparation of the Good News of peace;* (Ephesians 6:15 WEB)

The imagery Paul uses here draws heavily from the Old Testament, where a person's "walk" or "way," symbolized by fitting one's feet, describes the way he lives his life. The Gospel, or Good News, is that Jesus has come and taken upon himself the penalty for our sin by shedding his blood on the cross so we may be redeemed and have eternal life. This brings peace between us and God and also makes peace possible with one another. When you are grounded in the truth of the Gospel, you will march forward with confidence and be prepared to speak this peace into the lives of the people God brings across your path.

> *above all, taking up the shield of faith, with which you will be able to quench all the fiery darts of the evil one.* (Ephesians 6:16 WEB)

The devil has a great arsenal of "fiery darts." He'll throw at you all kinds of attacks, threats, losses, temptations, fear, accusations, and schemes to nerf you and gank you. He'll isolate you from your wingmen so it's easier to pwn you. A shield of faith might not instill confidence in you like holding a physical weapon in your hands might, but you have to remember you're up against a spiritual foe, not a physical one. Don't underestimate the power of faith to protect you. Paul isn't merely talking about your belief that Jesus is the Messiah, but also about how you trust the Lord and depend on him to win the battles for you. With that kind of faith, you can show Satan and his comrades there won't be any ganking you without them having first to pwn the Lord God Almighty!

> *And take the helmet of salvation, and the swovd of the Spirit, which is the word of God;* (Ephesians 6:17 WEB)

We know that a helmet protects a soldier's head, but we are up against **"spiritual forces of evil"** (Ephesians 6:12 ESV). Salvation is guaranteed to the believer who puts his faith and trust in the work of Jesus on the cross. Yet, Satan and his allies aim their schemes at our minds and hearts to nerf us and gank us. They will bring about circumstances and experiences that discourage us and cause us to doubt God's love for us and even our salvation, which is closely tied to our faith and trust in God. But when we have given God authority to transform and renew our minds (Romans 12:2), and we *"take every thought captive to obey Christ"* (2 Corinthians 10:5 ESV), then we can more easily reject doubts and deceptive philosophies, and Satan will find it very difficult to lead us astray.

Paul says the sword of the Spirit is the Word of God. In the previous chapter, Gaming the Instructions, we looked at Hebrews 4:12 and discussed how the Word of God is sharp, living and active, and discerning and judging. It is both a defensive weapon and an offensive weapon. A soldier would be foolish to head into battle without a breastplate, belt, shoes, helmet, and shield, but he stands a chance. However, a soldier who heads into battle without a sword is doomed. Likewise, the Bible is absolutely necessary for a Christian.

God's Word not only trains and transforms the believer, but the Christian can also use it to defend himself. Jesus used God's Word to thwart Satan's temptations (Matthew 4) and to win debates against the religious elites (Matthew 19, Mark 12, Luke 20). Peter and John used God's Word to defend themselves before the Jewish Council (Acts 4).

God's Word is the truth that challenges all the untruths in our culture today. God's Word is also the truth we can stand on when the enemy feeds us lies about ourselves, our salvation, and our circumstances. Knowing the Word of God helps us identify the lies and half-truths the enemy places in our minds.

Paul wrote all this about the armor of God to believers like you, who would inevitably face many faith-rocking challenges, trials, and temptations, but he didn't write them from a cushy office. You might not realize Paul wrote this from a prison cell. He was facing the same spiritual battle that he was writing about, and look how he continues:

> *with all prayer and requests, praying at all times in the Spirit, and being watchful to this end in all perseverance and requests for all the saints: on my behalf, that utterance may be given to me in opening my mouth, to make known with boldness the mystery of the Good News, for which I am an ambassador in chains; that in it I may speak boldly, as I ought to speak.* (Ephesians 6:18-20 WEB)

Paul could have commanded the church in Ephesus to pray he would get out of prison or to remove the chains from his wrists, ankles, and throat. Instead, he asked, like Peter, John, and the disciples in Jerusalem did, for boldness in speaking God's Word while enduring his trials. He had already put on the kind of armor that would help him thrive despite challenges, not escape them.

WHAT'S IN THEM

Before Jesus was crucified, he told his followers that he would send a Helper — the Holy Spirit to dwell in them.

> *I will ask the Father, and He will give you another Helper, that He may be with you forever; that is the Spirit of truth, whom the world cannot receive, because it does not see Him or know Him, but you know Him because He abides with you and will be in you.* (John 14:16-17 NASB)

The Holy Spirit dwells in us when we place our faith and trust in Jesus and enter into a covenantal relationship with him (Acts 2:38, 1 Corinthians 12:13). This Helper is present with us always, comforts us, guides us spiritually, gives us understanding (John 16:13), and produces the fruit of the Spirit in us (Galatians 5:22-23). When you know that he who is IN you is greater than he who is in the world (1 John 4:4), and you trust him, you'll naturally become more resilient. Nothing this world can throw at you will shake your faith in God Almighty (Psalm 23:4, Romans 8:18). Satan and his minions can do as they please.

You have little to no power in and of yourself that can withstand your spiritual enemies. This news makes many churchgoers bristle and fidget in their seats; no one wants to be weak. But here is the good news about that fact: the One who is in you is the shield around you and who strengthens you (Psalm 28:7). He is the One who goes with you through the waters and the fire and the One who will bring you through (Isaiah 43:2).

You can rely on your gaming XP and skills when you're up against the boss in an RPG, but you will need to buff your spiritual XP and skills with the DLC of God's Word, prayer, and daily drawing from the power of the Holy Spirit to overcome the schemes of the *"spiritual forces of wickedness in the heavenly places"* (Ephesians 6:12 NASB). Don't try to game Satan on your own strength. He is savvy and powerful enough to gank you with one arm tied behind his back, but he is no match for the One who dwells within you (Romans 16:20, Revelation 20:10).

With the Holy Spirit dwelling in you, you have the ultimate Wingman to help you through all the levels of life. You will also become a wingman yourself, helping others through their issues, transitions, and life challenges.

DISCUSSION & REFLECTION

1. Think of a solid Jesus-follower you could ask to be your wingman. Discuss these questions in the group:

   ✗ What do I need my wingman to know about me?

   ✗ _____

   ✗ _____

   ✗ _____

   ✗ How do I hope my wingman will help me?

   ✗ _____

   ✗ _____

   ✗ _____

   ✗ What are some ways I can help my wingman?

   ✗ _____

   ✗ _____

   ✗ _____

2. What kind of people do you spend the most time with?

    ⚔ Are **they** of the caliber to lift **you** up? Or do they bring you down?

    ⚔ Are **you** of the caliber to lift **them** up? Or do you bring them down?

    ⚔ What changes do you need to make that may catalyze growth in you and the people you associate with?

    ⚔ _____

    ⚔ _____

    ⚔ _____

    ⚔ How hard would it be for you to make these changes?

    ⚔ How can accountability buff your efforts to make these changes?

3. Describe a time when you were disappointed in God. (See Psalm 73:13)

    ⚔ What were your expectations of God in that situation?

    ⚔ Are you still disappointed? Why or why not?

    ⚔ _____

4. Is there a particular piece of the Armor of God that you
   need to begin using or use more?

   ◢ _____

   ◢ _____

5. What schemes or "fiery darts" has the devil fired at you?

   ◢ How did you recognize them?

   ◢ Describe how you overcame them.

6. How might you respond with spiritual weapons to the trial
   or situation you are currently facing?

   ◢ _____

   ◢ _____

[13] Pwned is pronounced "poned" - like "owned" only with the p at the beginning.

CHAPTER SIX

GAMING IT ALL

Your typical RPG has a main quest. Perhaps you must save yourself, your family, your community, or the world from monsters, dragons, gangs, or the coming apocalypse. Whatever the main quest happens to be, it's usually easy to know where you need to go. You may have a map with a highlighted path, or perhaps a compass or markers to guide your way through each phase of the game's primary mission.

In addition to their main quests, RPGs often have side quests. Sometimes, these secondary activities are necessary to gain XP or obtain items essential to complete the main quest, but getting wrapped up in side quests can be a major temptation. They can be fun and alluring, but you can waste a lot of time in maze-like corridors and hit dead ends while ignoring the game's main point.

Christians, too, can find themselves wrapped up in side quests that distract them from the main quest. Our pride, lust, and greed cause us to entertain ambitions, perspectives, lifestyles, and goals that divert us from the way the Lord desires for us. Those diversions may seem fun or alluring, but they bring serious dead ends and ambushes into our lives.

This book's themes are all about what being an authentic follower of Jesus Christ looks like. Look at how Jesus wrapped up the Sermon on the Mount. Jesus told us:

> *Enter through the narrow gate; for the gate is wide and the way is broad that leads to destruction, and there are many who enter through it. For the gate is small and the way is narrow that leads to life, and there are few who find it.* (Matthew 7:13-14 NASB)

We've heard these verses so many times that we can easily gloss over them. It's crucial for us to recognize that you enter through the gate first, and then you walk the way. Most people believe they must walk the straight path to get through the gate. But that's not what Jesus said. Jesus began this section of his teaching this way because it affects how we understand the rest of the message. Jesus said:

> *Not everyone who says to me, 'Lord, Lord,' will enter into the kingdom of heaven – only the one who does the will of my Father in heaven.* (Matthew 7:21 NET)

This shocks us because he is referring to people who confess Jesus as Lord. But he clearly says some have done that who will not enter the kingdom of heaven. This not only shocks us, but it seems to contradict what we read elsewhere in the Bible. Paul wrote, for example, in Romans 10:

> *... if you will confess with your mouth that Jesus is Lord, and believe in your heart that God raised him from the dead, you will be saved.* (Romans 10:9 WEB)

You may ask me, "What do you make of this contradiction?" I will tell you that there is no contradiction.

When you receive Jesus as your Lord and believe him in your heart, you will confess it and be saved. In his letter to the Roman Christians, Paul told them their relationship with Christ isn't a religion where they have to do certain deeds and rituals to garner God's favor (Romans 3 and 4). You are saved through your faith (Ephesians 2:8), which means you believe in God and trust him. Paul was pointing out, much like Jesus did, that you enter the gate and then walk the way. If you believe in Jesus and trust him (that's entering the gate), then you will love him, obey him, live for him, and do his will (that's walking the way).

Back to Matthew 7, Jesus said:

> *Many will tell me in that day, 'Lord, Lord, didn't we prophesy in your name, in your name cast out demons, and in your name do many mighty works?'* (Matthew 7:22 WEB)

When Jesus mentions "that day," he is referring to judgment day, and that makes us nervous. Some of you are thinking, "Well, I've never prophesied or done anything that would be considered a mighty work, so I'm not even as good as these people. What hope is there for me?"

There is plenty of hope for you. The good news is you don't have to cast out demons or perform mighty deeds to be saved. But it's essential to see that these people called Jesus "Lord." If you are reading this book, you have likely called Jesus Lord, too. These people served in various ways. You may have served in various ways, too.

But then Jesus said:

> *And then will I declare to them, 'I never knew you; depart from me, you workers of lawlessness.'* (Matthew 7:23 ESV)

These people thought they were "good" with God, but on judgment day, they discovered otherwise. And it's just so stark! Maybe it's because they seem like us. We confessed Jesus as Lord and served, too. But Jesus told them, *"I never knew you."*

How could Jesus say he never knew us?

In our modern-day lingo, we sometimes distinguish between knowing who someone is and knowing him personally, but we can say we know someone even though we may have never met him. In the Bible's languages and cultures, however, knowing someone is a more profound concept than merely knowing who he is. When Jesus talks about knowing someone, he's referring to a relationship. Jesus knows who everyone is! God even knows the hairs on your head (Matthew 10:30)! But that doesn't mean he has a relationship with you.

In 1 Samuel 15, the prophet Samuel tells King Saul that Yahweh has commanded him to lead his troops into battle against the Amalekites and utterly destroy them all: men, women, children, and livestock. Saul did war against the Amalekites and gained the victory, but he did not destroy them all. Saul let King Agag live and kept much of the livestock.

> *Samuel came to Saul; and Saul said to him,*
> *"You are blessed by Yahweh! I have*
> *performed the commandment of Yahweh."*
> *Samuel said, "Then what does this bleating*
> *of the sheep in my ears, and the lowing of*
> *the cattle which I hear mean?"* (1 Samuel
> 15:13-14 WEB)

Saul explained he thought it was a good idea to save some of the best animals so they could sacrifice to Yahweh. In fact, Saul insisted to Samuel that he had obeyed God. Samuel answered Saul:

> *"Why then didn't you obey Yahweh's voice,*
> *but took the plunder, and did that which was*
> *evil in Yahweh's sight?"* (1 Samuel 15:19
> WEB)

If we look at this verse out of context, you might get the impression that all you have to do is mess up once, and it's over between you and God. But look at what happened.

Then Saul said to Samuel, "I did obey the voice of the LORD, and went on the mission on which the LORD sent me, and have brought back Agag the king of Amalek, and have utterly destroyed the Amalekites. But the people took some of the spoil, sheep and oxen, the choicest of the things devoted to destruction, to sacrifice to the LORD your God at Gilgal."

Samuel said, "Has the LORD as much delight in burnt offerings and sacrifices as in obeying the voice of the LORD? Behold, to obey is better than sacrifice, and to heed than the fat of rams. For rebellion is as the sin of divination, and insubordination is as iniquity and idolatry. Because you have rejected the word of the LORD, He has also rejected you from being king." (1 Samuel 15:20-23 NASB)

Saul did not obey God's command. He did some of it, all right, but he had his own ideas about what should be done. Saul had wrapped himself up in a side quest. The way he replied to Samuel gives us the impression he thought he was doing God some kind of favor. God didn't want a favor - he didn't need sacrifices or offerings. God wanted Saul, but Saul withheld himself from God.

So when we hear Jesus say that only the one who does the will of his Father in heaven will enter the kingdom of heaven (Matthew 7:21), he is, in no uncertain terms, saying that when you receive him as your Lord and King, then his Word becomes your treasure, and his ways and his point of view become your ways and your point of view. However, some who claim to be Christians have deceived themselves.

When Jesus said, *"I never knew you"* (Matthew 7:23 NASB), his statement meant he had no relationship with these people. None of us wants to hear Jesus say that to us!

Several keys in the Sermon on the Mount help us understand what Jesus was getting at. This verse speaks to the core of what it means to be an authentic Christian. It's hard for me to consider authenticity as a follower of Jesus Christ without giving serious attention to what Jesus says in this context.

You have to do the will of God the Father, but how can you do someone's will? Well, when your boss tells you to do something, you have learned his will, and you do it. Of course, you might obey because you don't want to get fired. You can obey your boss without being loyal to him or adopting his vision or point of view. We understand this because all of us have had bosses who are fallible. That's why we don't worship them as our saviors or kings.

But Jesus Christ is not fallible. He is perfect in holiness, righteousness, power, and wisdom. When you receive Jesus as Lord, he doesn't just become your Savior. He becomes your King. You become his loyal subject when you declare that you believe in him and confess him as your Lord. Then, whatever is important to him becomes important to you. His Word becomes your treasure, his ways and his point of view become your ways and your point of view.

Of course, you might confess Jesus as Lord and get baptized merely because you don't want to go to hell. Some churchgoers obey without being loyal to Jesus or adopting his vision or point of view. Doesn't this have "side quest" written all over it? We all understand not wanting to go to hell. But I will tell you, just as clearly as Jesus told us all, no automatic formula provides you with a get-out-of-hell-free card.

NPCS AND BOTS

In role-playing games, players often interact with NPCs (Non-Player Characters), who aren't actual players but in-game characters programmed to serve a specific function. An NPC may have a minor, scripted role, whether it's a bartender in a tavern, a companion for part of a quest, or a maintenance man on a space station.

Other NPCs have just one function. Maybe they dance in the background or attack players, but they don't interact with them in scripted roles like other NPCs do. Some distinguish these simpler NPCs as Bots.

NPCs often have names and are character-like in that players may interact with them. They can contribute a lot to the game by giving clues and other information to the players, but they don't accomplish anything meaningful like the actual players do.

I liken NPCs and bots to those who say, *"Lord, Lord, did we not prophesy in Your name, ... and in Your name perform many miracles?"* (Matthew 7:22 NASB). You see, these are people who confessed Jesus as Lord. They were in church and served, much like NPCs are in the game and serve in some capacity. These people sometimes helped move things along like NPCs do in games. But the most sobering detail here is that these people are surprised they're not getting "in" like they expected. And this is the part we find so menacing. Some of you are thinking, "Hmm, I think I'm good with God, but what if I'm wrong? How do I know?"

Is it enough to say, "I believe that Jesus is the Christ," and then get baptized? Look: People who trust Jesus surrender to him, confess their belief, and get baptized. People who don't really surrender to Jesus but just want to avoid hell also make the confession and get baptized. People who surrender and trust Jesus serve in various ways. People who don't really surrender or trust Jesus serve, too. Saying, *"Lord, Lord,"* confessing, getting baptized, and serving don't automatically mean you're saved and good with God. But people who are saved and are good with God do those same things.

Non-player characters just go through the motions. They will follow a script (religious rituals and traditions, for example) but without authenticity in their words, actions, and intentions. Religious rituals and traditions are typically beneficial to the church community, but NPCs often perform them to "check off boxes" or to present themselves in a positive light in the church community. In this way, rituals and traditions can become side quests that derail us.

Many churchgoers believe in the automatic stuff. "All I have to do is repeat this prayer, get dunked, and I've got my stairway to heaven!" I haven't actually heard anyone use those words, but it certainly is what some believe. It is the perspective of someone whose side quest has caused them to disregard the main quest.

Sometimes, Christians believe that they just need to be moral. Although a true follower of Jesus will be moral, it's not enough to be a moral person. Face it, half of the unbelievers you know are unbelievers because they met up with a so-called Christian who knew "about" Jesus and may have been very "moral" but didn't know Jesus well enough to be loving, kind, humble, or even honest. You know churchgoers like that. I've even known church elders like that.

Likewise, although a true follower of Jesus will often be in God's Word, reading God's Word doesn't automatically make you a true follower of Jesus Christ.

I want you to think about your relationship with Jesus. Remember, that's what God is looking for. That's what he desired with King Saul. It's what he has sought with his creation since the beginning. He told his disciples, "Follow me," and they dropped their livelihoods and followed him.

Are you one who does the will of God the Father? Have the things that are important to him become important to you? Has his Word become your treasure? Have his ways and his point of view become yours?

If you ask why you have to adopt his ways as your own, you might be an NPC or a bot. He is the Creator — you wouldn't exist without him. Jesus is the Sovereign King. He has declared what is good and right. Many others, wooed by the evil one, have made millions of contrary suggestions about what they think is good and right, but all those ways lead to destruction.

Jesus is also the Savior. No other divine, sinless, and holy being loved you so much that he gave his life to pay the penalty for your sin, only Jesus. Therefore, you can only have this unique relationship with him by entering his gate and walking that narrow path.

Let's say there's some misbehavior you routinely do — getting plastered, lying, flirting with other people when you're married, or whatever — and then a brother or sister confronts you about it. God has called him as your wingman - your DPS in this case - to warn you. He is using that brother like a sword or chisel to detach that sin from you. So what will you do? Will you get angry and try to justify what you've been doing? Or will you let God cut away the sin that is dragging you into the abyss?

Let's say you're reading God's Word and you see how the Israelites gave at the temple, what the book of Proverbs says about generosity, what Jesus says about giving, or what Paul writes about giving to the church. Then, you hear a mission organization urging you to be generous at offering time. What will you do? Will you fold your arms and say, "Nothing doing, my money is MY money," or will you let God soften your heart so money won't have such an idolatrous hold on you?

Let's say you're getting ready to go fishing or hunting. Or maybe you're getting stoned or drunk, I don't know. But then, your boss calls and asks why you're not at work. You put on a raspy voice and tell him, "Oh, I don't feel so well today; I don't think I can make it." What will you do when you see that stare your children are giving you? Will you holler at them to mind their own business, or will you let God's sword sink in so he can carve that liar out of you?

You see what I mean? Followers of Jesus possess an openness to his Word, to his teaching, to his truth, and to his light that NPCs and bots do not. People who want just enough Jesus to stay out of hell unwittingly throw themselves into it.

I don't want to frighten you or make you doubt your salvation, but I do want you to be candid with yourself. When you repent of your sin, confess Jesus as Lord, and get baptized, you become what the Bible calls "sanctified." The Bible describes sanctification in two ways.

First, sanctification means you become holy and set apart (Hebrews 10:10, John 17:16-18, 1 Corinthians 1:30). It's a one-time phenomenon. After entering into a covenant with God through faith in Jesus, God considers you righteous and holy and will not hold your sins against you. But your sanctification does not mean you're perfect. You will still sin and struggle with issues and shortcomings.

Second, the Lord then begins the ongoing process of sanctification (Hebrews 10:14 and 12:14, Philippians 1:6, 2 Peter 3:18). You will grow in wisdom and understanding as you spend time in God's Word, in fellowship with other Christians, and put your faith to work in your life. God will gradually smooth your rough edges through your Bible reading, interactions with others, and changes in your circumstances.

When you become a Christian, you don't automatically know everything about God's will and what is important to him. You might not immediately treasure his Word or adopt his point of view. Such perspectives and understanding take time and work before they penetrate deep down into your worldview.

Authentic followers of Jesus are not perfect in knowledge, wisdom, and behavior. They are, however, on that narrow road where they are open to his Word, his teaching, and his truth, and also sensitive to his light in ways NPCs are not.

You don't want to be a non-player character, just in church but not part of the church. Perhaps you're a churchgoer who is okay with looking like a Christian but not very good at having a relationship with Jesus Christ. You've done and said some of the right things, so you look like you belong, but you might be an NPC.

Look with me at what Jesus said in verse 24.

> *Everyone therefore who hears these words*
> *of mine, and does them, I will liken him to a*
> *wise man, who built his house on a rock.*
> *The rain came down, the floods came, and*
> *the winds blew, and beat on that house; and*
> *it didn't fall, for it was founded on the rock.*
> *Everyone who hears these words of mine,*
> *and doesn't do them will be like a foolish*
> *man, who built his house on the sand. The*
> *rain came down, the floods came, and the*
> *winds blew, and beat on that house; and it*
> *fell—and great was its fall.* (Matthew 7:24-
> 27 WEB)

These two houses both had curb appeal. What was the
difference? The foundation!

The wise man knew to build his home's foundation on the rock.
Even though it was much more difficult, he did it. When the
rains, floods, and winds came along, he endured.

The foolish man also knew what to do, but he had his own
ideas about how to get it done. That house fell, and it was
catastrophic.

King Saul knew what he was supposed to do, but he had his
own ideas about how to get it done. King Saul fell, and his fall
was dreadful.

If you know his Word is to be your treasure, and his ways and his point of view are supposed to be your ways and point of view, but you have your own ideas about how to live your life and get it done, great will be your fall.

You don't want that. And I don't want that for you. If you thought all you had to do was a little of this and a little of that, and God ushers you through the Pearly Gates, you might be as surprised as these NPCs Jesus talked about at the end of the Sermon on the Mount.

This chapter's content is pretty sobering. Like I said, it isn't my intention to make you fearful or make you doubt your salvation. Many communion meditations encourage us to examine ourselves. A primary reason is that we can deceive ourselves just as easily as Satan can. Lust, pride, greed, and other sins create a slippery road for us. It's easy for us to slide into a rut or a ditch.

No authentic relationship is cultivated by accident. Living as an authentic follower of Jesus is not an accidental life but an intentional one.

When you surrender to Jesus, it's not a surrender like you might do before an enemy. When you surrender like that, you're just trying to save your life, but all the while, you hate, resent, and rebel. NPCs and bots do that with Jesus — they are gaming it all, and they may lose it all.

When you surrender to Jesus, you receive him as your Lord and Savior, entering the gate and becoming his. Then, you walk with him on the path where he will bring his Word, his teachings, his commands, and his ways to bear on your life. He will work through other believers, his Word, and your circumstances to begin his transforming work in you: a transformation you will not find or see in bots.

DISCUSSION & REFLECTION

1. Do you recognize non-player character features or behaviors in yourself?

   ✗ _____

   ✗ _____

   ✗ _____

2. Recount a time a "wingman" confronted you about your behavior. How did you respond?

    a. I rejected what they had to say.

    b. I accepted what they had to say and turned things around.

    c. I initially rejected what they had to say, but later accepted.

    d. Other. Explain.

3. Describe a time when God used circumstances to confront you about a behavior.

    a. Was it clear to you that the circumstances and the behavior were connected?

    b. Did the situation cause you to change that behavior?

4. How does sin create a slippery road for us and make it easy to slide into ruts?

5. How open would you say you are to God's Word, his teaching, and his truth?

    a. Very open.

    b. Fairly open.

    c. Not very open.

    d. Closed.

6. Think about one intentional change you'd like to make in your journey with Jesus Christ. What steps can you take to turn this intention into a reality?

    ✎ _____

    ✎ _____

7. Has your emphasis as a Christian been on avoiding hell or becoming a better citizen of God's Kingdom?

8. Think about a recent decision you had to make.

    a. Did you approach it as someone building on the rock? Or on the sand?

    b. How did your faith influence your decision? Or did it?

CHAPTER SEVEN

GAME OVER

HIGHWAY HYPNOSIS

I was driving through Illinois once when I missed my exit because I received a perfectly timed phone call. I realized my mistake very quickly and began trying to correct my route. Two exits I needed were closed for construction, and another had a detour. It seemed like forever before I made it to the proper highway.

Culturally and spiritually speaking, it's unsettling how smooth and seamless it can be to miss our exit and continue barreling in the wrong direction. We are immersed in this wayward culture. Hearing the same songs, mantras, and slogans day after day makes it easy to adopt them into our lingo and even into our thinking. We fall victim to what Driver's Ed class called highway hypnosis. The monotonous, unceasing patterns of painted lines, mile markers, and blurred pavement mesmerize the driver, who becomes inattentive to his surroundings.

Our modern, "enlightened" culture has a limitless supply of "adds" (additional enemies) to toss your way to gank, nerf, tilt, and discombobulate you. The movers and shakers in our society are yelling, whispering, and singing to us to pass up our exits. How easy it is to game everything once we're coasting downhill in the wrong direction like everyone else.

Many churchgoers give themselves and others the impression that they are faithful believers but have unwittingly taken God off the throne of their lives and put something else in his place. And when I say unwittingly, I refer to that highway hypnosis phenomenon. They have been mesmerized by the blurring overabundance of sweet-sung slogans and entertaining images in our culture. Those conflicting messages from other "software" make churchgoers inattentive to fellowship in church life, the truths in God's Word, and the war between good and evil we find ourselves in.

The world is constantly trying to grab us and turn us aside. In addition to the innumerable sports and entertainment options that distract us, there's no end to the deafening chatter we hear from the world. Follow your feelings; follow your heart; follow your dreams; if it feels good, do it. You just need money. You won't be happy if you're not going viral. Follow your truth! Follow your team! Follow the latest TV show!

Networks, politicians, and influencers woo us to respond emotionally rather than rationally. We tend to obey our culture's siren songs, accepting those slogans instead of thinking about them critically. The truths, principles, and traditions of our faith then fade in our minds and hearts because it is so easy to touch a screen and flood ourselves with the culture's vivid messages.

We have that highway hypnosis phenomenon going on in our culture. Behaviors and attitudes that were unthinkable a few decades ago have become accepted and must now be cherished and promoted. Mesmerized by the slogans and songs, we keep passing up our exits.

If you realize you've been going in the wrong direction, you have a choice. You can either continue down that same destructive road or get off and work your way to the proper highway. Stop gaming life. It's time to say GAME OVER.

CAMPING

When a player routinely hangs out or hides in the same place in a game, waiting for a predictable event or character to come along, it's called camping. They remain stationary, repeating the same moves over and over. Gamers often camp to frustrate other players, gain an advantage over them, or perhaps rack up extra points.

It's quite easy to fall into the habit of camping when it comes to church or our faith. Churchgoers don't necessarily do this to frustrate or gain an advantage over other people, but they will hang out in the same place, going through the routines they always do. Their walk of faith gets whittled down to repeated moves: go to church, greet some people, get coffee and doughnuts, sit, stand, sing, sit, listen, greet, leave.

When we were in Africa, we decided to help an amputee who I routinely saw begging at the market. We sent him to a special clinic where he received surgery to correct a deformity from his original amputation. After some healing and therapy, he was to be fitted for an inexpensive prosthetic leg that would permit him to walk again. Instead, he disappeared from the clinic. I couldn't imagine what would make a lame man turn away from the ability to walk again.

I saw him begging in our city's market a few months later. I asked him what had happened. He explained that no one would give him alms if he had received this artificial leg and could walk again. Therefore, he would be expected to work and earn a living for his family. Not only was it easy to beg, but he sometimes received more money by begging than he could earn from a job.

My amputee friend in Africa was disheartened by the idea of changing something he had been accustomed to for so long. A whole new life could have been his, but he settled for the familiar routines. It was easier for him to camp.

It's the same for churchgoers. Many can't imagine an authentic relationship with Jesus, but he has not made it difficult for us to have that. Still, our churches have an abundance of soft Christians gaming it all today. They are suffering from that highway hypnosis. The world's persistent enticements tempt Christians to take their faith and traditions less seriously, and that makes it easier for them to camp. Or, those worldly enchantments tempt Christians to twist their faith into something it shouldn't be for the comfort of acceptance in the culture.

SHORTCUTTING

In our RPGs, we're accustomed to button combinations or keystroke sequences to help us double-jump, run faster, use a special technique with our weapon, or do special kicks. We may try shortcuts and workarounds when we game church, too. Even though Rusty believes in Jesus, he feels that taking his faith more seriously is unnecessary. He has his own interests and ambitions and isn't interested in disrupting them by operating with Jesus' interests and values in mind. He'll go through the button combinations at church (greeting people, sitting, standing, singing, listening), but all it does for him is give the appearance that he's Christian when he is, in fact, using the wrong apps and loading the wrong skins.

Although few churchgoers voice it this way, many believe that attending church earns them points with God just as it earns them some social standing with their church community. Rusty's perspective is that he can live as he likes during the week, but he ensures he stays on God's good side by going to church on Sunday mornings. Instead of letting God's Word and the Holy Spirit influence his ethics at work or his attitudes and behavior at home or at play, he continues as an NPC at church while living a secular life everywhere else.

We have everything to lose if we are gaming God. As long as we are content to play Christian in the church building, like first -person shooters in a role-playing game, we could wind up being those people Jesus told, *"I never knew you. Away from me, you evildoers"* (Matthew 7:23 NIV), and we'll be just as surprised as they were.

To many, surrendering to Jesus seems daunting. You might think I was wrong when I said Jesus hasn't made having a genuine relationship with him difficult. You might be afraid you'll have to give up your fun, fearful of what your friends will say, or scared that walking closer with Jesus will threaten your lifestyle. We all have to come to terms with those things, but honestly, those activities and lifestyle choices are idols, not crucial needs. At the moment, they seem like the "I-gotta-have-this-or-life-ain't-worth-living" things because you're living in the highway hypnosis state.

Truth is what will help snap you out of it. We have all sinned (Romans 3:23), your sin puts a barrier between you and God (Isaiah 59:2), and the consequence of sin is death (Romans 6:23). Sin requires a blood sacrifice to cleanse it away and restore the relationship with God (Leviticus 17:11, Hebrews 9). That's why we read so much about the sacrificial system in the Old Testament. But Jesus, who never sinned, came to be that sacrifice for us. He took care of the hard part of belonging to him and having an authentic relationship. Romans 5:8 says:

> *But God demonstrates His own love toward us, in that while we were yet sinners, Christ died for us.* (Romans 5:8 NASB)

Because Jesus paid the penalty for our sins, God applies his righteousness to us through our faith in Jesus (Romans 3:22-24).

FAITH AND WORKS

The Apostle Paul advocated for faith in his letters to the churches he planted. After Paul left for other places, legalists came along trying to convince the new believers that they had to obey the Law of Moses to be Christian. Paul refuted that by explaining that a person is justified and saved through faith, not through his works. He declared that we don't become righteous in God's sight by obeying (Romans 3:20); we obey because God has made us righteous. Unfortunately, some people took this to mean that all you had to do was believe — you didn't have to do any works at all.

The Apostle James contended with that misunderstanding. He didn't contradict Paul; he developed Paul's argument a bit further.

> *For as the body apart from the spirit is dead,*
> *so also faith apart from works is dead.*
> (James 2:26 ESV)

James told us that when you have genuinely placed your faith and trust in Jesus, you will live that faith out. He emphasized that it is an authentic faith that bears fruit. We may look to Paul's description of the fruit of the Spirit in Galatians 5:22-23 to define that, but James generalized.

James wanted us to understand that a Christian who has placed his faith and trust in Jesus will, according to James chapter 2, follow Jesus' teachings and do good works. This implies something more profound is happening inside the believer than just an intellectual or emotional agreement that Jesus is the miracle-working Messiah.

And something profound is indeed going on. Jesus illustrated this in his Wineskins Parable.

> *Neither is new wine put into old wineskins.*
> *If it is, the skins burst and the wine is spilled*
> *and the skins are destroyed. But new wine is*
> *put into fresh wineskins, and so both are*
> *preserved.* (Matthew 9:17 ESV)

In the Ancient Near East, wine was made by putting grape juice in a leather bag called a wineskin. As the grape juice fermented, the gasses produced would stretch the leather. Once wine was made and consumed, that wineskin would become rigid and couldn't be used to make more. If someone tried to make wine again in the same wineskin, the rigid leather would not stretch when fermentation began. Instead, the leather would crack and split, and the wine would leak out.

Jesus always preferred painting a picture rather than merely giving us facts. In this parable, he tells us that his way is a radical new way of life in faith that is incompatible with the old ways. Faith in Christ isn't something you can merely add to whatever beliefs and religious system you currently favor.

When we learn something new in a game (how to double-jump, for example), we add that new data to the information we already have: how to change weapons, secret ammo stash locations, and so on. But faith in Jesus is not new info that we can simply add to the other information we already possess: Jesus isn't going to co-exist with your current idols.

IDOLS, YOU SAY?

Like adding new wine to old wineskins, many churchgoers just add Jesus to their existing perspectives, beliefs, and desires. Everyone wants to be saved, but not everyone wants to be redeemed and transformed. They don't mind adding Jesus to what they've got going on, but they don't want him governing their perspectives and ambitions. They believe they can have Jesus and still enjoy their idols, but this brings conflict into their lives. Jesus warned his disciples about this:

> *No servant can serve two masters; for either he will hate the one and love the other, or else he will be devoted to one and despise the other. You cannot serve God and wealth.*
> (Luke 16:13 NASB)

Jesus mentions "wealth" here because he was talking about money and treasure in the presence of the Pharisees, who were lovers of money. If money is your idol, you may feel safe when you have sufficient income, savings, and investments. As soon as your wealth is threatened, you will panic and start scrambling to save your idol.

And there are plenty of other idols besides wealth. As I pointed out in Chapter 6, many believe in God and have confessed Jesus as Lord, but other gods have captivated their hearts. Navigating through life, whether in the church building or out, is usually smooth until something threatens the idol.

Wealth is a big one, but we also live in a culture where attractive people become celebrities, so everyone wants to be beautiful. But what if you aren't attractive? Or you're getting older and your beauty is starting to head south? Or you have to be successful, but you're just meh? Or fashionable, but you've got Wal-Mart? Or shapely, but you're chunky? What will you do?

If you lack any of these idols that are so prevalent in our culture, then you might feel worth less. That's what idols do to you. Our culture convinces us these idols are essential for our happiness and fulfillment. But they cannot redeem you, save you, fulfill you, or make you happy. As soon as they are threatened, you'll fall apart. Why is there so much stress wrapped up in your idols? I mean, it is so easy to become obsessed with attaining them, maintaining them, and trying not to lose them. Here is a sobering thought: those idols will always drive you to love them and sacrifice for them, but they will never love you or sacrifice for you.

A NEW CREATION

Jesus is entirely different. He did sacrifice for you. Jesus loves you so much that he went to the cross to pay the penalty for your sin. When you place your faith and trust in him, entering into a covenant with him in baptism, he saves you and begins the renewal process. In other words, he comes in and starts cleaning house, freeing you of the idols shackling you to old addictions, bad habits, and destructive thinking.

Jesus' renewal process is revolutionary because the Gospel is revolutionary. No other king, president, or lord has given his life for yours. Only Jesus. And the Lord of the heavens and the earth will not content himself with your camping worship on Sunday morning, nor should anyone expect him to, because our salvation takes place within a covenantal relationship with Jesus.

> *Therefore if anyone is in Christ, he is a new creation. The old things have passed away. Behold, all things have become new.* (2 Corinthians 5:17 WEB)

When Paul describes us as "in Christ," he is expressing the state of being in a covenantal relationship with Jesus. This relationship is described in numerous ways in the New Testament including becoming children of God (John 1:12, Romans 8:16, 1 John 3:1-2) and living stones in God's spiritual temple (1 Peter 2:5). Entering into this kind of relationship with Jesus is akin to being adopted as sons (Romans 8:15), and changing our citizenship (Philippians 3:20), and not merely adding a little Jesus who sits alongside our ambitions, hopes, and dreams.

The Gospel does not merely mean we add worship services to our lives. It radically changes our behavior because it radically changes how we think. We have become part of God's Kingdom and embrace Kingdom values and priorities that are utterly different from the mindsets the world promotes. The world teaches us to hold grudges, get revenge, hate our enemies, and do the minimum required, but Jesus has taught and lived out forgiveness, going the extra mile, and loving one's enemies, even praying for them.

As a new creation, you stand out. It makes a radical difference in who you are whether you are in a church building or somewhere else. Living out your faith everywhere you go is something that happens when your life has been transformed from the inside out.

When your avatar bites the dust in an RPG, you'll spawn: come back to life ready to get back at it. We don't get too many replays in life. But you have a matchless opportunity with Jesus. The old you dies, and a new you emerges — respawns, as it were. Look how Paul described it in Romans 6.

> We were buried therefore with him by baptism into death, in order that, just as Christ was raised from the dead by the glory of the Father, we too might walk in newness of life. (Romans 6:4 ESV)

When your game character respawns, you come back with the same skin and are pretty much who you were before, although your features and weapons are often nerfed or downgraded to their initial state. However, when you are **"born again"** (John 3:3, 1 Peter 1:3), you aren't nerfed, and you are not who you were before. You are a new creation.

A problem afflicting many believers is assuming that getting saved or being born again is the destination. That's not true. Churchgoers who fall into this erroneous belief wind up gaming life, church, and God. They'll often go AFK (Away From Keyboard) because they either think that no further commitment or activity is necessary or because they have changed as much as they want and are avoiding further discomfort in the transformation process. But getting saved is only the beginning of the journey. Christ desires full surrender, not just when deciding to become a Christian, but also in the ongoing process of becoming more like him.

Becoming like Jesus requires us to abide in him. Jesus said:

> *I am the vine, you are the branches; he who abides in Me and I in him, he bears much fruit, for apart from Me you can do nothing.* (John 15:5 NASB)

Sadly, we modern English speakers don't use the word "abide" much anymore, but it's excellent for translating the Greek word here, which means to dwell, reside, or remain. To "abide" in Jesus means much more than a casual friendship. The vine and branch imagery that Jesus used gets that across to us. Looking at a grapevine, it doesn't appear very active, but there's a lot more going on than meets the eye. The branch receives all its nourishment from the vine, but only if it is one with the vine. If you cut a branch off of a grapevine, that branch will look fine for a little while. But the leaves will start shriveling hours later and all turn brown by the next day. Jesus' listeners knew this and understood that "abiding" meant you had to have a very close and faithful dependent relationship with him. Somehow, we need to be one with Jesus so that we receive nourishment from him.

We need the DLC of God's Word as frequently as possible. Why? The nourishment we draw from him is necessary to keep us alive, thrive in our faith, and bear fruit. The world's siren songs don't stop when you become a Christian. They get louder and more alluring. The slogans are ricocheting everywhere. God's Word helps build our spiritual immune system and enables us to defend ourselves against the enemy who wants to distract and destroy us.

Read the Bible or get an app that will read it to you, but get that content in you, somehow. Even if you have a hard time understanding it or don't know how what you're reading fits in the bigger picture, getting it into you will have its effects. God's Word guides us and does indeed help us to navigate through this topsy-turvy period of time we call life. But you have to get it in you.

We also need frequent fellowship with brothers and sisters with a mature faith. Rubbing elbows over coffee and doughnuts before the service begins won't cut it. Serious time studying God's Word together, having fun together, helping one another, tackling community projects together, and visiting one another are akin to game controllers in God's hands as he works to mold us and shape us into who he wants us to be.

The Apostle Peter wrote:

> *You also, as living stones, are built up as a spiritual house, to be a holy priesthood, to offer up spiritual sacrifices, acceptable to God through Jesus Christ.* (1 Peter 2:5 WEB)

There is much more to being in Christ and following him than doing the camping routines in a church building. You become one with your Creator, part of an infinite kingdom and plan, serving an infinite God. Our lives here on earth are extraordinarily short, no matter how old we become. God has invited you to come under his covenantal authority and love and to embrace his transforming power.

The Bible teaches you the explicit truth about how to belong to him. It teaches you to turn away from the sins, idols, and false truth claims you've adhered to. It teaches you to surrender to him to be reconciled to God and be adopted into his family. It teaches you how to abide in him. It teaches you how to live radically differently than you used to. And if you are a follower of Christ, it teaches you the clear truth about your ultimate destiny.

> *And I heard a loud voice from the throne saying, "Behold, the dwelling place of God is with man. He will dwell with them, and they will be his people, and God himself will be with them as their God. He will wipe away every tear from their eyes, and death shall be no more, neither shall there be mourning nor crying nor pain anymore, for the former things have passed away." (Revelation 21:3-4 ESV)*

The truths in God's Word wake us up, sober us, and encourage us. They draw us into a deeper relationship with the Lord, less deeply into our selves, and thus more apt to see this world's truth claims for what they are — power grabs.

I pray that you recognize all the ways you may have been Gaming Life and decide to say GAME OVER. Through abiding in Jesus Christ and his Word, you will put your NPC and camping days behind, beat the boss, become resilient like a tank, and be salt and light in an ever-darkening world.

GL HF DD.

DISCUSSION & REFLECTION

1. What behaviors, attitudes, or habits have you been accustomed to for so long that the idea of changing them seems daunting?

2. What are the reasons you go to church?

   ✗ _____

   ✗ _____

   ✗ _____

   ✗ _____

3. Do those reasons correspond to the three elements of spiritual health from Chapter 1 (worship, discipleship, service)?

4. What, if anything, makes you nervous about taking your faith in Jesus more seriously?

    a. It seems unnecessary.

    b. It will make me unpopular in my circles.

    c. I don't want to be associated with churchy people.

    d. I don't want to give up activities I enjoy.

    e. I want to avoid ridicule.

    f. Changing old habits is very difficult.

    g. I've committed too many sins for such change to do me any good.

5. Discuss the consistency between your faith and your behavior.

    a. Does your faith influence your daily actions and decisions?

    b. Share an example of a situation where you feel your behavior aligned well with your faith principles.

    c. Have you developed any practices or habits that help you live out your faith in Jesus?

    d. What do you or can you do when you feel your faith and your actions or decisions are at odds?

6. An idol refers to anything that becomes the focus of our devotion instead of God. Are there idols that you wrestle with?

Here are some prevalent idols:

  a. Material possessions and wealth.

  b. Self-image and success.

  c. Comfort and security.

  d. Power and control.

  e. Technology and entertainment.

  f. Religious rituals and traditions.

7. Identifying and addressing our idolatry requires self-reflection, prayer, and a commitment to aligning one's heart and priorities with Jesus' teachings and values. What steps can you take to minimize the influence idols have on you while maximizing the influence Jesus has on you?

✗ _____

✗ _____

✗ _____

✗ _____

AND THERE'S MORE...

If you found that *Gaming Life* motivated you to apply your faith to your whole life, you may be interested in **THE CATALYZER.**

Just a little bit of friction will light a match. That match can then light your campfire, enabling you to stay warm and cook an amazing feast. Or that match can light a fuse that ignites a rocket or kicks off a chain of events.

You might recognize that your faith-walk is lacking – nearly everyone is in that boat. You admire those guys who are knowledgeable, prayerful, and resilient. You may think you can't get to that point, but little additives in your daily habits can open the door for the Lord to bring about big transformations. Just adding a little friction can light your fire.

Subscribe to the Catalyzer newsletter or work with Jim by visiting The Catalyzer website at:

https://catalyzerbook.com/

Join The Catalyzer Facebook Group at:

https://facebook.com/groups/1650988108781885

Made in the USA
Monee, IL
02 November 2024

68510119R00094